Afghan Cuisine
Cooking for Life

A collection of Afghan Recipes (and other favorites) for the Novice Afghan and non-Afghan cook
By: Nafisa Sekandari

ISBN: 1-4033-8589-0 (e-book)
ISBN: 1-4033-8590-4 (Paperback)

Library of Congress Control Number: 2002095170

This book is printed on acid free paper.

Printed in the United States of America
Bloomington, IN

1stBooks – rev. 01/21/03

Table of Contents

Forward

I want to start off by saying I am not a chef nor would I ever consider myself to be one. In saying that, I believe that if I can cook Afghan food, anyone can. The purpose of my putting this book together was to translate favorite Afghan recipes that I grew up with to English, so that I, along with other Afghans (and non-Afghans alike) could learn to cook Afghan food without having to call our mothers every other second. This book is as much for me as for the reader. As a child, learning to cook meant having to cook dinner all the time, and I was not interested in that kind of commitment. I stayed out of the kitchen until I moved out on my own to go to college. At that time, I was a vegetarian and did not eat much except salads, baked potatoes with plain (non-fat) yogurt, and spaghetti. Cooking was not difficult. Being a college student, I often ate out at cheap restaurants with my friends. Cooking was not important. Also living alone, I didn't need to make anything extravagant. I would quickly put something together, just so I wasn't hungry. I was caught in a double bind however, because typical American food (with the exception of fast food and restaurant food) was not familiar to me (I ate my first sandwich at the age of 23) but I couldn't cook Afghan food. [Prior to becoming a vegetarian, I would only eat hamburgers, when I would eat out.] I didn't have the ingredients and didn't know where to begin. I was content with my salads, baked potatoes and spaghetti dinners. My dinners were simple. I didn't like cheese and didn't eat meat or eggs. As I grew older and the time away from home grew longer, I began craving certain Afghan dishes. The foods I really liked however were simple as well. My mom often made fun of me because my favorite foods were what was considered peasant food in Afghanistan (because they were all meatless dishes). I began putting my own recipe's together that were a mixture of western and Afghan cooking. My meals continued to be quick. I usually didn't have time to wait an hour for a meal to be cooked. Over the years I've learned that many of the dishes can be prepared in less than half an hour, if you are prepared and become more skilled. My mom has taught me many time saving techniques that have really helped. For example, I always have a container of frozen minced garlic in my freezer. I also have a container of frozen fried onions, frozen minced ginger, and frozen vegetables. Even big containers of tomato paste can be frozen to save time and money. My mom also cooks some dishes ahead of time and freezes them until needed. This trick really helps when unexpected guests (as is often the case with Afghans) drop in. Because I used to live too far from Afghan bakeries, I would also buy large amounts of Afghan bread and freeze it. The bread usually lasted me about 1 semester, usually the amount of time I'd be away from home. Around the age of 25, I began cooking more Afghan dishes, but didn't know how to adjust the recipes for 1 person. I would end up eating the same dish for a week because I would usually make too much. When I moved to Pasadena, my neighbors started coming over my house more often and I'd share my cooking with them. It was through them that my experiments and desire to cook started. My neighbor and friend, Claudia, and I would take turns cooking for each other. She'd cook Mexican dishes for me and I'd make Afghan food for her. She began making requests and I became more confident in my cooking. One year I became brave enough to invite friends over to celebrate my birthday, and I made Afghan food. I made Qabli Palau, Chalau, quarma's (vegetarian), and Banjan Bourani. I got all the recipes from my mom of course. To my surprise they liked my cooking and asked for recipes! I then wanted to collect more recipes for the future and got the idea to write a cookbook. When I was in Tortola, British Virgin Islands, I made Shour Nakhud (page 22) to take along with us when we went sailing. On the boat I met other tourists and we started talking about my cookbook. They were very unfamiliar with Afghan food. After a few hours of swimming, I brought out the Shour Nakhud and served it to all. It was an instant hit and they all promised to buy the book when it was done. I hope they remembered and make good on their promise!

When I began taking on this project to write a cookbook and preserve my mother's recipes, I didn't know what I was getting into. First of all I didn't know the first thing about writing a cookbook. I started checking out cookbooks from the library and reading how recipes were written. I would also watch the food networks and watch chefs cooking. I began collecting several cookbooks and before I knew it, cooking became an obsession of mine and I learned much about cooking in the process. What I found to be even more difficult than writing a cookbook, was trying to translate my mom's recipes in a measurable manner. It is the Afghan custom to not measure anything but put "a little bit of this, and a pinch of that". I would watch my mom, and other relatives and try to quantify the ingredients and put the process in easy to follow steps. I would also try to catch my mom in her limited spare time and ask her to recall her recipes. Because I knew she was estimating many of the ingredients, I started to have "Afghan cookbook parties" while I was living in Pasadena. I would give my neighbors and co-workers (all non-Afghans) recipe's to follow and then ask them to bring the dish to the party to be tasted and evaluated. It was through these parties that the recipes became measurable. I wanted to test the recipes prior to publishing the book, to make sure they could be easily followed by young Afghans and non-Afghans alike. I also included many Afghan relatives (experienced and inexperienced cooks) in my parties to be "judges" of the dishes in order to give me a different perspective. My friends that tried the recipes were completely foreign to Afghan food. It was reassuring to hear positive comments about the food and recipes. All expressed interest in getting their hands on this book, which motivated me to work on it even more. Unfortunately due to working and dealing with the daily life situations, I didn't have the time to dedicate to completing this book. The book was to be completed by December 1999, as part of my family's 20th anniversary of our escape from Afghanistan. It also took me a long time to gather recipes and compile them together in this book due to my mother's busy work schedule and my distance away from her. I moved back to the Bay Area on July 2001, which gave me more opportunities to be apart of my mothers cooking.

As I was writing this book, I wanted it to be more than just a cookbook. At the time, the women and children in Afghanistan were being tortured by the Taliban. There wasn't much help, and many countries pulled out their humanitarian aide due to Human rights violations by the Taliban. I desperately wanted to help out the poor women and children that were reduced to begging in Afghanistan. I wanted to finish the cookbook and go on the Oprah Winfrey Show to talk about the needs of the Afghan women and children. I wanted the world to know that the images of the Afghan woman that was seen on T.V. is not what the religion dictates nor was it a typical image of the Afghan woman. Prior to the invasion of Afghanistan by the Soviet Union, women held high positions in the Government, Universities, Schools, and Banks. Women were teachers, doctors, lawyers, and nurses. Education is highly stressed in Islam and in Afghanistan. As Prophet Muhammad (pbh) said "seek knowledge from the cradle to the grave". My grandmother traveled to Turkey to receive an education in the early 1930's because at that time Turkey had one of the best educational systems. At the age of 70, she borrowed my children's English dictionary and began teaching herself to speak English. So to see women being deprived of education, forced into hiding, begging , becoming prostitutes, committing suicide, and selling their children for food was very heartbreaking for me. Only women that are forced to live under such extreme conditions would go against their religion, morals, beliefs, and upbringing to do what is necessary for survival. The emotional damage that was done to these women over the 23 years of war is irreparable. There is no way any of us living in the west, and having never been in a war like situation, could relate to what these women went through. Many survived hunger, poverty, rape, physical and emotional violence, grief, and constant fear. After September 11th, the women received the much needed media attention and the Taliban were overthrown. But the need continues to be there and I still want to help. I intend to send a portion of the sales of this book to help the women and children of Afghanistan but I also hope to go there personally and deliver the money and my time to support them in any way I can. There is still a great need in the areas of medical and education for women and children. Afghanistan continues to be very much a part of my life. It breaks my heart to see the women and children suffer and there is little I can do. I have supported humanitarian efforts in Afghanistan for the past 10 years but it never seems like enough. Now that there is a new administration in Afghanistan, I want to participate in rebuilding my homeland in anyway I can and I hope with the proceeds of this book, I can make a difference somehow.

Acknowledgements

I would like to dedicate this book to my mother for providing me with the recipes and inspiring me to preserve them through her delicious cooking. I would also like to dedicate this book to my father for being such a creative cook and for his willingness to experiment with recipes and spend time with us cooking and baking. His creativity and interest in cooking has inspired me to want to learn to cook. I would like to thank my relatives, friends, neighbors, and co-workers that have participated in my "Afghan cookbook parties" and have given me feedback on improving the recipes. Also thank you for encouraging me to finish this book. I'd like to also thank my aunts and cousins that have been kind enough to assist me in my book by sharing with me their specialty recipes.

Cookbook party participants (June, 2001)
Left to Right: Hasina Shairzay, Claudia Roa, Kerlan Kim, Shirley Suen, Maria Rubalcaba, Harry Wong, Zarpan Osmani, Mariam Omadi, Diba Ghish with Author in the center.

About Afghanistan

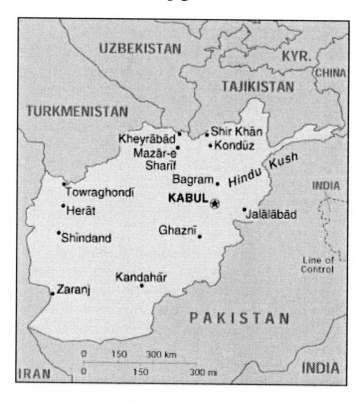

Afghanistan is a totally landlocked country about the size of Texas, with an extremely rugged topography. It borders Iran, Turkmenistan, Uzbekistan, Tajikistan, China and Pakistan, and is strategically important to all.

The mighty Hindu Kush mountain range, the western extremity of the Himalayas, runs across the country from east to west. The average elevation of this mountainous interior is a lofty 8856 ft and the highest peaks reach 24,600ft in the northeast. To the north of the Hindu Kush are the low laying plains of Afghanistan, Turkistan and the border marked by the Amu-Darya (Oxus). To the south stretches the dry, dusty Dasht-i-Margah, or Desert of Death.

Afghanistan's history as a country spans little more than two centuries, although it has contributed to the greatness of many great

Central Asian empires. As with much of the region, the rise and fall of political power has been inextricably tied to the rise and fall of religions.   It was in Afghanistan that the ancient religion of Zoroastrianism began in the 6th century BCE. Later, Buddhism spread west from India to the Bamiyan Valley, where it remained strong until the 10th century AD. The eastward sweep of Islam reached Afghanistan in the 7th century AD, and today the vast majority of Afghans are Muslim.

Due to the recent media attention about Afghanistan, there has been much covered about the country, the people, and the traditions. In no time in the past has Afghanistan received such media coverage. It was through this coverage that Afghanistan underwent such drastic changes over the past year.   The coverage encouraged positive changes to occur in the country and the issues of the women and children were brought to the attention of the world.

Kabul, the capital city, used to be a bustling city prior to the Russian Invasion of 1979. Today Kabul has little remaining from its historic past. The majority of historical landmarks have been destroyed over the 23 years of fighting. The city of Kabul today does not resemble the city of 23 years ago. Travel outside the capital is considered to be dangerous at this time. As of the writing of this book, there are many feuds among local warlords and fighting continues in the surrounding areas. In addition to the continuing civil strife, the country suffers from enormous poverty, a crumbling infrastructure, and widespread land mines.

Despite the war, hospitality and guests remain very important to the Afghan people. Even though the people living in Afghanistan had very little to eat themselves and a few were forced to sell their own children for rice or flour, they continued to share what little they had with guests.   This is because hospitality and guests are a very important part of the Muslim religion. There is always an open door policy in regards to guests with Afghans and Muslims. Afghan food is a big part of the tradition and customs of Afghanistan. It is the center of every family gathering and the main part of social occasions. Food is so important to the Afghan people that it is said that a wedding is judged by how good the food was. Afghan food is a blend of cooking styles from Iran and India as well as from the many groups of invaders that have invaded and occupied Afghanistan throughout the centuries. Afghan food is a delightful cuisine that is neither too spicy nor too bland. Afghans traditionally include meat in most of their recipes. The meat used can be lamb or beef. Afghans, being Muslim, do not eat pork or pork product. The meat is usually "halal" which means that the animal needs to be slaughtered a certain way. In the Muslim manner, that means that a prayer asking God for permission ("In the name of God the most compassionate, the most merciful") is said prior to slaughtering the animal at the throat. This is believed to be the best way to drain the blood and prevent bacterial growth and the most painless and humane way for the animal to die.

Afghan specialties include Palau and kabobs. Quarma's (stews/sauces) are served with Chalau (white basmati rice). Afghans also eat a large selection of fresh fruits and vegetables.

Tea is an important part of Afghan cooking and is served after every meal. Afghans usually drink black tea with cardamom but the trend in the United States is changing to green tea. Sweets are often served with tea. Afghan deserts are not very sweet but are perfect served with tea. Noqul (chickpeas and almonds covered with sugar and spices) and Qand (sugar cubes) are usually served to guests at family gatherings and weddings. There are also a variety of cookies, pastries, and candies. Nuts (almonds, walnuts, pistachios, etc.), dried fruit, raisins, and chickpeas are also served with tea.

Afghan Bread (Nan) is also a major part of the life of Afghans. Afghan bread is very versatile and can be used for breakfast, lunch, or dinner. It can be used to spread jam and butter on, or eaten with eggs and potatoes. The bread resembles a long pizza without the toppings (pg. 124). Afghans in the United States used to bake their own breads but due to the major effort it requires to make the bread and the wide availability of the bread in Afghan grocery stores, it's easier now to simply buy it. I have never met anyone that does not like Afghan bread, especially when it's fresh out of the oven.

Getting Started

I organized the book in what I think is an easy to follow order and tried to make the recipes easy to follow. I also included many non-Afghan dishes that have come to be my favorites over the years, for variety. I don't think this is a traditional Afghan cookbook. I think there are many traditional home style Afghan cookbooks out there, but I wanted mine to be a book for the person that doesn't cook often, is interested in learning how to cook Afghan food in a simple manner, and wants to blend the East and the West in one book. Afghan cooking has a tendency to use a lot of oil in the dishes, so I reduced the oil amount in my recipes but if you want your food to be oilier, increase the amount and if you want less, decrease the amount. My frustration with traditional Afghan recipes is not only the amount of oil in the dishes, but the variety of recipe's that are difficult to follow here in the United States. I included most of the favorite recipes, retained the traditional flavor, but included some short cuts and common ingredients that are easily found in the United States.

Time Saving Tips

- Frying large quantities of sliced onions ahead of time and freezing it saves a lot of time in dishes such as Aush, Kitchiree Quroot, and Palau. You can use what you need as you need it.
- Mincing large quantities of garlic through a meat grinder and freezing it also saves a lot of time. Use when needed and put back in freezer. I don't like the store bought variety due to added preservatives and taste.
- Pressure cookers are often used in Afghan cooking and reduce the time of cooking.
- The Azumaya brand pasta wraps are great substitutes for dough recipes in such dishes as Aushak, Boulani, and Mantu. There are different variations available at the local grocery stores such as: Large square Pasta Wraps (eggroll wrappers) used for Boulani, small square pasta wraps ((wonton wrappers) used for Mantu,

and round pasta wraps (potstickers and dumpling wrappers) used for Aushak.

Afghan cooking takes practice and patience. Not too many dishes can be prepared in a rush. The quarma's take time and the ingredients can be tempered with to suit individual tastes. My spice measurements might be too much or not enough depending on the individual. I've learned to play with it and put in what I think is enough, but then I see my mom put in so much more and it always comes out good. So don't be afraid. After a few times of cooking, you will strike a perfect balance and be able to "put in a little bit of this and a pinch of that".

Oil: I use only Extra Virgin, cold pressed, olive oil in my cooking (with the exception of frying) but regular vegetable oil is often used in Afghan cooking.

Pots: Afghan cooking comes out best in good quality pots and pans. Non-stick pots are o.k. for quarmas but a heavy based pot is better. Basmati rice does not come out well in non-stick pots because you don't get the "Ty-Digi", or the crust on the bottom of the rice, once it's cooked. The pots do not need to be expensive but should be good quality and heavy duty. I used to wonder why every Afghan relative I knew had the same pots and pans along with platters, but I realized that the cooking requires it.

Herbs and Spices most commonly used in Afghan Cooking

Most of these herbs can be found in your local grocery store or health food stores. The herbs and spices that are specific to the Afghan/Asian region can usually be found in Afghan, Iranian, or Indian grocery stores.

Ab-e-Gulab (Rose Water): Used in Halwa, Firnee, Shirbirinj, and other deserts.

Bodiyan (Anise): Related to cumin, caraway, dill, and fennel. Commonly used to aid in digestion.

Hail (Cardamom): Used in rice, deserts, and tea. Cardamom has a cooling effect on the body and considered good for all digestive disorders.

Dal Chini (Cinnamon): Used in rice, stews, and desert. Cinnamon is considered to be a strong stimulant for the glandular system and helpful with stomach upsets.

Dona-e-Kunjid (Sesame Seeds): Sprinkled on bread and rhote. Sesame seeds are very nutritious. They contain a lot of protein and make a great addition to all kinds of dishes such as salads, stir-fry, or pastries. Sesame seeds also have many medicinal properties.

Gashneez (Coriander): Cilantro seeds usually ground and used in quarmas, rice, and meat dishes. Coriander is often used to aid digestion and the seeds are a mild sedatives used to ease migraines. In India, the powder is a basic ingredient of the curry powder.

Gundana (no English equivalent available): Long flat leaves that look like long grass. Gundana is difficult to find in the United States;

unless you grow your own, which my mom did using seeds she bought from an Afghan store. If you can't find Gundana, you can substitute leeks or scallions instead in recipes. Used fresh in Aushuk, Boulani, or salads.

Holba (Fenugreek): Used in Spinach quarma. Medicinally, it is used to reduce blood cholesterol and good for diabetes. Also considered a hair-growing stimulant.

Kosh-Kosh (Poppy seeds): The seeds are sprinkled on breads and cookies.

Mikhak (Cloves): Used in Palau and other dishes. Cloves are considered to be a powerful antiseptic.

Murch-e-sabz (Green chili Peppers, also known as jalapeno's (fat green peppers) or Serrano Peppers (thin, long green peppers): The green chilis are used in salads soups, quarma's, chutneys, and tourshies (pickled vegetables).

Murch-e-surkh (Red chilies): The Red chilies are either fresh or dried, which are either used whole, crushed, or ground. Usually good for tourshies and quarmas.

Murch-e-sia (Black pepper): Used in most afghan cooking. The alkaloid found in pepper stimulates the saliva and gastric juices, killing bacteria, improving the appetite, aiding digestion, reducing flatulence, and nausea. Also good for constipation and diarrhea.

Namak (Salt): Used in most dishes as well as salads, breads, and drinks.

Nahna (Mint): Used fresh or dry (crushed) in dishes, salads, and yoghurt. This herb is also known to aid in digestion and has a cooling effect on the stomach.

Palau mix: 1 tablespoon of cinnamon, 1/2 teaspoon of cloves, cumin, and cardamom.

Pudina (Pennyroyal): A wild herb grown in Afghanistan, and used like dried mint and sprinkled over Aushuk, Aush, and yoghurt.

Raiyan (Basil Seeds):   These little seeds can be found in Afghan grocery stores or you can extract the seeds from the basil plant. The seeds are well hidden so the process of extracting the seeds can be very tedious. These seeds are used to make this very refreshing drink that is served at weddings, parties, and funerals. It consists of 1 tablespoon of seeds, 1 teaspoon of rosewater, and sugar (to taste), mix in jug of water and serve.

Seer (Garlic): Used in most Afghan dishes, including marinades, and tourshies.

Shibit (Dill): Used in soups, rice, and spinach quarmas. Dill has a reputation for being a great aid to digestion.

Sia Dona (Black Seeds) (Nigella): Used in various dishes, cookies, rhot, and bread.   This herb also is used to aid in digestion and good for treating stomach and intestinal problems.

Zaffron (Saffron): Used in Palau's and Chalau's. Also used in some deserts. Saffron is a very expensive spice. It is very expensive to produce and it takes 20,000 stigmas to produce one pound of saffron. Only very small quantities are used in dishes and deserts. It is believed to be beneficial for fever and cramps.

Zanjafeel (Ginger): Used ground or fresh in various dishes. Ginger has a warming effect on the stomach and used to soothe indigestion.

Zard choba (Turmeric): Used in many afghan dishes. Turmeric has a strong flavor and should be used in moderation. Considered to be a good aide for digestion.   Research has shown that turmeric strengthens the gallbladder, inhibits dangerous blood clotting, reduces liver toxins, and helps the liver metabolize fats and therefore aids weight loss.

Zeera (Cumin): Used in Chalau and Palau. Said to be good for iron absorption. Used mostly in ground form unless specified. For Chalau, whole cumin is mixed with the rice right before it's steamed.

Other common ingredients in Afghan dishes

Alou Bukhara (Bukhara Plum): This is the plum usually found in Bukhara. Found mainly in Central Asia but can be bought in Afghan and Iranian grocery stores. Used dry in quarma's like meatball.

Banjan (Eggplant): This can be the regular eggplant or the Japanese size eggplants. Used in quarmas and Banjan Bourani.

Banjan Rumi (Tomatoes): These are the typical, common salad tomatoes but roma tomatoes, along with other tomato varieties can also be used. Used in salads, quarmas, soups, etc.

Birinj (Extra Fancy long grain Rice): This is usually Basmati rice used in Chalau's and Palau's.

Birinj-e-Luk (Long grain rice): This rice is used in dishes like Kitchiree Quroot. Although the name implies long grains of rice, it's actually shorter than the basmati rice kernels.

Dal (Dal): A split pea used to make the dish Dal. Dal is easily found in Indian grocery stores as well as Afghan stores.

Dal Nakhud (Split Peas): Used in quarmas, soups, and shami kabab.

Lobiya (Red Kidney Beans): Used in soup and quarmas. Can use canned beans or dry.

Kachaloo (Potatoes): Basic brown Russett potatoes used in soups, quarmas, Kachaloo Bourani, and Boulani.

Nakhud (Chick Peas/ Garbanzo Beans): Used in various dishes, including aush, soups, and shour nakhud. Can use canned chickpeas (Garbanzo beans) or dried.

Maush (Mung beans): Green split pea type beans used in Kitchiree Quroot and Maushawa.

Piaz (Onion): Used in almost all quarmas, soups, kabobs, Kitchiree Quroot, and Palau, among other dishes.

Rhub-e-banjan rumi (Tomato paste or puree): Used in almost all quarmas, soups, Palau, Kachaloo Bourani, etc.

Measurements

4 cups = 1 Quart
4 Quarts = 1 Gallon
3 Teaspoons = 1 tablespoon
4 tablespoons = ¼ cup
16 tablespoons = 1 cup
15 pounds = 1 Cir of Kabul (Afghan measuring system)
16 ounce = 1 pound
1 cup = 8 ounces
2 ounce = ¼ cup
1 ounce = 300 grams
1 cup of flour = 150 grams
1 cup of sugar = 200 grams
1 tablespoon of flour = 25 grams
1 tablespoon of oil = 20 grams
1 pound of dry beans = 2 dry cups of dry beans = 6 cups of cooked
cup of beans
9-10 egg whites = 1 cup
1 pound of dry rice = 2 cups of dry rice = 6 cups of cooked rice
1 pound of sugar = 2 ¼ cups
1 kilograms = 1000 grams
1 man = 8 Cir of Kabul

1 gal=4 qt=8pt=16 cup=128 fl oz=3.79 liter
½ gal=2qt=4 pt=8cup=64 fl. oz.=1.89 liter
¼ gal=1 qt=2 pt=4 cup=32 fl. oz. = .95 liter
        ½ qt=1 pt=2 cup=16 fl. oz.= .47 liter
        ¼ qt= ½ pt=1 cup=8 fl. oz.= .24 liter

Quroot and Yogurt

Quroot

Quroot is a ball of very dry afghan "cheese" made from drained, salted, and dried yoghurt. To prepare quroot for serving with particular dishes, the ball is soaked in hot water and then in a blender made liquid. Quroot can be bought in Afghan stores nowadays but the recipe is as follows.

1. Put 1 quart of sour yogurt in a pot and bring to a boil. Allow to boil for 2-3 minutes and remove from stove.
2. Add about ½ cup of salt, more if needed to make it salty but not too much.
3. Line a colander with cheesecloth and put yoghurt in colander. Bag up the cheesecloth and tie a knot. Hang the cheesecloth over the sink and allow to drain.
4. Once drained, take out the yoghurt and make small balls out of drained yoghurt. Place balls in a tray and set in the sun for a few days until they become hard.
5. Store the dried balls in a cool dry place. They will last a long time. Use as needed.

Mahst (Homemade Yogurt)

Afghan yogurt, "Mahst", is very rich and sharp in taste. It is served plain or with chopped cucumbers and dry mint.

Note: For your first batch of homemade yogurt, use plain commercial yogurt (look for one with no preservatives) as your starter. From then on, save at least ¼ cup from your last batch as the starter for your next.

Also important:

- All utensils used in making and storing yogurt must be sterile.
- It is essential to use only very fresh whole or 2% low fat milk.

- Check the temperature with a dairy thermometer or a built in thermometer spoon available at houseware stores. If you can dip your little finger into the warm milk and count slowly to 10 without burning your finger, the milk is ready.

1 quart whole or 2% low-fat milk
¼ cup plain yogurt starter

1. Place milk in a heavy saucepan and bring to a boil. Simmer for 2-3 minutes.
2. Remove from heat and set aside to cool to 120 degrees F or until the milk feels comfortably warm to your little finger or when dropped on your wrist.
3. Put the yogurt starter in a small bowl and stir in about ½ cup of the lukewarm milk until the starter is completely dissolved. Add the yogurt mixture to the remaining lukewarm milk, stirring gently to blend.
4. Pour into a glass dish with a lid. Put the covered container on a baking sheet in an unheated oven or cover them with clean dry towels and place in a warm, draft free part of the kitchen. Let stand undisturbed until the yogurt is set, about 6-8 hours. The lower the percentage of fat in the milk, the longer the yogurt will take to set. And the longer it sets, the more tart the yogurt.
5. To store, refrigerate, covered, for up to 1 week.

- Optional: Use ¼ cup non-fat dry milk and mix well with regular milk until dissolved in a saucepan and bring to a boil. Heat mixture over medium heat to 180 degrees F or until bubbles begin to appear around the edges and a skin forms on top. Stir the skin into the mixture. Follow steps 2-5 above.

Doughe (yogurt drink)

A refreshingly cool drink especially during the hot summer days.

1 cup yogurt
1 pitcher of ice water
Salt to taste
A pinch of mint
1 cucumber (peeled and chopped finely)

Place the yogurt in a pitcher and beat into a paste. Gradually add the water, stirring constantly. Add salt, mint, and cucumber. Mix well and chill. Serve in glasses. Add a sprig of fresh mint on the glass as garnish (optional).

Chaka (Fresh Yogurt Cheese)

1 teaspoon salt (or more to taste)
1 quart plain yogurt
Cheese cloth bag or sheets (10"X10")

1. At least one day before serving, gently stir the salt into the yogurt.
2. Line a colander with 4 single layers of cheesecloth. Pour the yogurt into the cheesecloth. Gather the corners into a bag and tie them together securely with a cord.
3. Hang the bag over the kitchen faucet high enough to drain into the sink, or suspend over a deep bowl (you may leave the yogurt to drain in the colander, however suspending it allows a better drain and results in a firmer, more creamy curd.) Let it drain overnight or until the yogurt curd is firm. The texture should be the consistency of softened cream cheese. Remove from the bag and place in a container.
4. Sprinkle salt and dry mint over it and serve.

5. To store, refrigerate, covered, for up to 1 week.

*   Makes about 1 quart. Can be spread on bread, or with tomatoes, and cucumbers. Eat for breakfast, lunch, or dinner. Also makes a good dip for chips and can be a good substitute for sour cream.

Chaka in a store bought container:
Buy 1 quart of commercial yogurt and stir in ½ teaspoon of salt. Pierce the bottom of the container in several places with a sharp fork. Place the container in a colander and let the yogurt drain until all the whey is removed and the curd in the container is firm and spreadable. Season as desired. Refrigerate, covered, for up to 1 week.

<u>Qaymagh</u>

This is a thick cream that is usually eaten for breakfast with bread and sugar sprinkled on it. It is very good but can only be eaten every once in a while since it's so fattening.

1 quart Half and Half cream
½ cup milk

1. Put one cup of half and half in a saucepan and heat over medium low heat. Stir cream constantly so it doesn't boil over or burn. Once it thickens (about 15-20 minutes), remove and place in a bowl. Keep doing this until all the cream has thickened. Keep removing thickened cream and place in bowl. Once 1 cup is thickened, add additional cup and repeat process until the entire quart is thickened.
2. Place thickened cream in a bowl and allow to cool.
3. Add ½ cup of milk over cream and refrigerate
4. Serve with warm toasted Afghan bread and sprinkle sugar on top.

Side Dishes
(Salads, Chutneys, Tourshies, etc.)

Salata (Salad)

Afghan food always has a vegetable or yogurt "Maast" supplement. The Afghan salad, "Saa-la-ta", is a simple combination of fresh Tomatoes and onions chopped into small rectangles. The salad is always topped with fresh squeezed lemon and cut cilantro or fresh mint. Since the ingredients are fresh the traditional Afghan Salad makes a delicious supplement to the food. Remember Afghan salad is eaten WITH the food -- not before or after the meal.

Hummus

This dish is not Afghan but goes well with Afghan Bread. Hummus is rich in protein and taste. This recipe was given to me by my co-worker Maria.

2 cans of chick-peas (15 oz. Each)
3-4 big tablespoons of tahini sauce
3-4 cloves of garlic
½ to 1 teaspoon salt
Juice of 1 lemon
Black pepper
¼ cup of water

1. Drain the chickpeas and place in a food processor.
2. Add tahini sauce, garlic, salt, lemon juice, water, and pepper and blend until smooth.
3. Add additional salt and lemon juice as needed.
4. Serve with pita bread or traditional Afghan bread.

Baba Ganoush

This is also not an Afghan dish but Afghans do have a similar dish to Baba Ganoush called Burta. This also goes well with Afghan Bread. This recipe was also given to me by my co-worker Maria.

2 eggplants
4-5 cloves of garlic (sliced)
2-3 tablespoons tahini sauce
½ teaspoon salt
Juice of 1 lemon
Black pepper
¼ cup of water

1. Wash and cut eggplants in half.
2. Stud half pieces of eggplant with slices of garlic (stick garlic inside eggplant meat and skin).
3. Bake or broil eggplant for 5 minutes.
4. Once eggplant is soft, take out of oven and let cool.
5. Stick eggplant, salt, lemon juice, pepper, tahini sauce, and water in a food processor and blend well. Add more lemon and salt as needed.
6. Serve with warm pita or afghan bread.

Shour Nakhud

This is an appetizer, picnic type of dish.

2 can of Garbanzo beans
1 can of kidney beans
1 cup of cilantro chutney
4-5 potatoes

Salt
Pepper
Crushed chili peppers
1 cup of apple cider vinegar

1. Wash potatoes with skin, put in a deep-dish pot, add a little bit of salt along with 5-6 cups of water and boil until cooked.
2. Drain and let cool.
3. Once cool, peel potatoes and slice them from top down in a big bowl. They should be thin, circular slices of potato.
4. Rinse Garbanzo beans and kidney beans and add to potatoes.
5. Add cilantro chutney, salt, pepper and chili peppers along with vinegar and mix.
6. Allow to chill in the fridge prior to serving.

Chutney Gashneez (Cilantro Chutney)

1-2 bunches of Cilantro (thoroughly washed)
2-3 cloves of garlic
1-2 Serrano chili peppers
1 cup of Apple Cider Vinegar
Salt to taste
¼ cup of walnuts (optional)

1. In a blender, blend the cilantro, garlic, peppers, and walnuts with ½ cup of vinegar.
2. Add more vinegar as needed to give it a liquid consistency. Add salt. Blend and taste.
3. Add more garlic, vinegar, or peppers as needed to make it the desired spicy level.

Chutney Murch-e-Surkh (Red Pepper Chutney)

4 large red bell peppers
6 small Red chili peppers (Skinny peppers)
1 cup Apple cider vinegar
One whole garlic bulb
6 oz. of tomato paste
1 teaspoon of Sia Dana (Nigella)
Salt to taste
1 tablespoon of sugar

1. Wash peppers and take out seeds.
2. Put in a blender along with vinegar.
3. Blend until pureed.
4. Put in a pot and boil for 5-10 minutes.
5. Liquefy tomato paste with a little bit of water and then add to pot.
6. Boil for 30-40 minutes and let cool.
7. Mince garlic and add with sugar, salt and sia dana.
8. Mix in pot and put in jars.
9. Seal jars when chutney is cool.

Tourshie Banjan (Pickled Eggplant)

The tourshie is a specialty of my aunt "Maggie" so I'm grateful that she shared her recipe with me. The following recipes are very different than the commercial pickled vegetables you get at the stores. I have not tasted commercial pickled vegetables as good as these, ever. I think it's the mint and nigella that are the secret ingredients.

3 lbs. Japanese Eggplant
1 bulb of garlic
1-2 tablespoons dried crushed red pepper

1 lb. mix of fresh red and green jalapeno peppers (the fat peppers)
Salt
2-3 tablespoon Sia Dana (Nigella)
2-3 tablespoon dried crushed mint
4-5 cups Apple cider vinegar

1. Select soft small Japanese eggplant.
2. Wash Eggplant and clip the green leaves from around the base.
3. Split the eggplant from the bottom to the base (lengthwise) but do not cut all the way through. Stop right before the base.
4. In a cooking pot, fill 3/4 way with water and boil the eggplant for 5-10 minutes until tender but not too soft. Drain the eggplant in a colander and allow to cool for a few hours (4-5 hours or overnight).
5. In a bowl mix the sia dana, mint, salt, and crushed red pepper.
6. Slice the garlic cloves thinly (use entire bulb).
7. In a jar big enough to hold all the ingredients, layer a few of the eggplants in a circle and then add a few jalapeno peppers over the eggplant. Sprinkle with spice mix and garlic. Continue this process alternating eggplant, peppers, and spice mix until all are in the jar.
8. Add vinegar in the jar and fill jar to about 1 inch above vegetable level.
9. Seal jar tight and allow to sit for 2-3 days.
10. After 3-4 days, it's ready to be served with your favorite dish such as Chalau and Quarma.

Tourshie Tarkari (Pickled Mixed Vegetables)

1 lb. Carrots
1 lb. Cauliflower tips

1/2 lb. Turnips
1 lb. mix of fresh red and green jalapeno peppers (the fat peppers)
1 bulb of garlic
1-2 tablespoons dried crushed red pepper
Salt
2-3 tablespoon Sia Dana (Nigella)
2-3 tablespoon dried crushed mint
4-5 cups Apple cider vinegar

1. Wash and peel carrots. Cut into quarters.
2. Wash and peel turnips. Cut into quarters.
3. Wash Cauliflower tips gently.
4. Fill a big pot 3/4 way with water and add carrots and turnips. Boil for about 5 minutes or until cooked. Add cauliflower tips and boil for an additional 2 minutes. Drain all vegetables in a colander. Allow to cool for 5-6 hours. [Vegetables need to be completely cooled prior to putting in jars, otherwise they will mildew).
5. In a bowl mix the sia dana, mint, salt, and crushed red pepper.
6. Slice the garlic cloves thinly (use entire bulb).
7. In a jar big enough to hold all the ingredients, layer a few carrots in a circle and then add turnips, and cauliflower tips, then add a few jalapeno peppers over the eggplant. Sprinkle with spice mix and garlic. Continue this process alternating vegetables, peppers, and spice mix until all are in the jar.
8. Add vinegar in the jar and fill jar to about 1 inch above vegetable level.
9. Seal jar tight and allow to sit for 3-4 days.
10. After 2-3 days, it's ready to be served with your favorite dinner dish such as Chalau and Quarma.

Tourshie Tarkari

Rice Dishes

Chalau (Steamed Basmati Rice)

Chalau is one of the main dishes in Afghan cooking.   It is very versatile and is served with the quarmas and fish dishes.

2 cups of white basmati rice
2-3 tablespoons of vegetable oil (more if you want your rice oily)
Salt
3-4 quarts of water for rice to cook in
1 clean cloth big enough to cover lid

1. Wash rice thoroughly until water runs clear, drain and add fresh water to cover rice.
2. Add salt (1-2 tablespoons) and let sit for at least 30 minutes to an hour (or longer).
3. In a deep-dish pot, fill midway with water.
4. Add 2-3 tablespoons of salt and bring to a boil.
5. Take ¾ cup of water from the pot and set aside.
6. Drain the rice and add to boiling water.
7. Stir the rice until it comes to a boil.
8. Check the grains for softness on the outside but the core should be a little hard. If it overcooks, it becomes sticky and mushy. It should not boil for more than 5 minutes.
9. Once the right consistency is reached, drain the rice in a colander and put back into pot.
10. Add the water set aside to the rice.
11. Add oil.
12. Mix and bring to a mound.
13. Put several holes in the mound with the end of the spoon.
14. Put the lid in the cloth and wrap the lid in the cloth. Tie a knot over the lid with the cloth to keep cloth in place. Place lid on the pot.
15. Turn heat on high until steam comes out from under lid. Then turn the heat to low and cook for about 20 minutes.
16. Take out rice and serve with any quarma.

Note: This dish becomes easier with practice.

First place the lid on the towel

Then wrap the towel around lid

Then place the wrapped lid on the pot

Palau, Chalau, Quarma, Banjan Bourani, and Shell Pasta

Qabli Palau (Rice with chicken, raisins, and carrots)

Palau is an old favorite Afghan dish. The number of ways Palau can be cooked depends on the chef's imagination. There are many variations of Palau including but not limited to: Sabzee Palau (Spinach), Yakhni Palau (with mutton in steamed rice), and Narinj Palau (orange peel and rice). I only included the chicken qabli palau here.

2 breasts of chicken (cut in half)
1 medium onion
3 cups of basmati rice
½ cup of oil
2 tablespoons of tomato paste
2 teaspoons cinnamon
1 teaspoon of cumin
1 teaspoon of ground cloves
1 teaspoon of ground cardamom
3-4 quarts of water for rice to cook in
1 teaspoon salt
2 carrots (julienned)
½ cup of black raisons

1. Wash rice thoroughly then soak in water, sprinkle 2 tablespoons of salt and allow to sit for 1-2 hours.
2. Spice Mix: In a container, mix the cinnamon, cumin, cloves, and cardamom. Set aside.
3. Slice onions, add with oil in a deep-dish pot and carmalize (brown and slightly crispy). Drain oil out in a separate bowl and grind onions finely to a pulp in the pot with a wooden spoon. Add the oil back in the pot, add tomato paste, and water. Boil for 3-4 minutes. Wash chicken and remove fat. Add chicken to the onions along with 1 tablespoon of the spice mix and a ¼ tsp. of

salt. Allow to cook for 15 minutes. Remove chicken from the pot and set aside. Drain the liquid from the mixture in a bowl using a mesh strainer. The leftovers in the strainer can be discarded. Keep the liquid and set aside.

4. Wash raisons and set aside.
5. In a small frying pan, add a small amount of oil and fry carrots for 1-2 minutes. Remove and set aside.
6. In a separate pot, add 3-4 quarts of water. Add salt to water and bring to a boil. Drain water from the rice and add to boiling water. Allow to boil for 3-4 minutes. Check rice by tasting one kernel and test whether it's al dente. Rice should be soft on the outside and slightly hard on the inside.
7. Drain rice in a colander. Place the drained rice back in the pot. Add ¾ -1 cup of onion liquid over the rice and mix. Add ½ teaspoon of spice mix over the rice and mix in with rice. Add more salt as needed.
8. Add Chicken in the center of rice. Pull rice over the chicken and form a mound. Put several holes in the mound with the end of the spoon.
9. Add carrots and raisins over the mound. Use a clean cloth to wrap the lid in and cover pot and cook on medium low for 30-40 minutes.
10. When ready, take ¾ of rice out in a big platter and separate the meat and carrots and raisins. Set aside. Put meat on the rice and cover with remaining ¼ of rice. Put carrots and raisins on top of the rice and serve.

Put meat on the rice

Cover meat with rice

Add carrots and raisins to rice

Kitchiree Quroot

This is my favorite dish. I only recently learned how to make it but I've been requesting this from my mom since I was a kid. Once my relatives discovered that I liked this dish, they would make it for me when I'd come over to visit.

¼ cup of oil
1 cup Birinj Luk (see ingredients list) wash and set aside for 1-2 hours
¼ onion (sliced)
¼ cup mung beans
3 quarts to a gallon of water
½ teaspoon of fresh or ground ginger
2 to 2 ½ teaspoons of salt
¼ teaspoon of black pepper
½ teaspoon coriander
1 cup plain yoghurt or Quroot
1-2 cloves of minced garlic
3 tablespoons of oil
1 whole jalapeno pepper
Dry mint

1. Wash rice thoroughly, and allow to soak in clean water for 2-3 hours. Wash mung beans thoroughly as well and allow to soak for 2-3 hours.
2. In a pressure cooker, carmalize onions. Add mung beans and water. Drain rice and put in pressure cooker along with corriander, salt, pepper, jalapeno pepper, and ginger. Cook for 10-15 minutes. Check to see if cooked. Add water and cook as needed.
3. In a frying pan, heat garlic in oil for 1-2 minutes until browned. In a separate bowl (make sure the bottom is clean), place yoghurt and add the oil and garlic over the yoghurt.

4. Take out the Kitchiree quroot and place in a platter. Insert the bowl of yoghurt and garlic mixture over the rice mound and serve. The yoghurt is poured over the rice. Can sprinkle mint if desired.

Alternative to pressure cooker:
- In a deep 5-quart pot, add oil and onions and caramelize.
- Add 2-3 cups of water along with the mung beans. Cook for 10 minutes with pot covered.
- Drain rice and add to mung beans along with remainder of water, corriander, salt, pepper, jalapeno pepper, and ginger. Mix in well and cook on low heat for about 40-45 minutes. Add more water as needed until rice is cooked.
- Follow steps 3 and 4 from above.

Quarmas (Stews)

I will admit that I have not personally made these quarmas with meat but I've made the vegetarian variety quite often. I have however dispensed a few of the quarma recipes to my non-Afghan friends to try out and the other guests at the Afghan cookbook parties have responded very favorably to the recipes. The idea of a quarma appears quite foreign to Westerners, but it's the basic staple of the Afghan meal. At my house, we eat different quarmas with rice on a daily basis. You put the quarma over your rice and eat. The Afghan way to use utensils is to use a spoon to eat with and use the fork to push the food into the spoon, so therefore you use both your hands. This method makes eating rice with quarma a lot easier than using only a fork.

Quarma (meat sauce base)

This is the base for all the quarma recipes. In some sections I've repeated this recipe but in others, it just refers back to this recipe. In some recipes, a few ingredients may differ from this recipe so be aware and follow the recipe given for the particular dish rather than follow this. Serve this and all quarmas with Chalau.

1 ½ lb. beef or lamb meat
½ cup oil
1 large onion, finely chopped
2 to 3 cloves of garlic, minced
1 ½ cup water
salt
Freshly ground black pepper
¼ to ½ teaspoon hot chili pepper
¼ cup yellow split peas (dal nakhud)
1 teaspoon ground cumin
2-3 tablespoons chopped cilantro

1. Cut meat into ¾ inch cubes.

2. Heat oil in a heavy pan, add onion and fry gently until transparent. Increase heat, add garlic and meat cubes and fry, stirring often, until juices evaporate and meat begins to brown.
3. Add water, salt, and pepper to taste, chili pepper, washed split peas, and cumin. Bring to a slow simmer and reduce heat. Cover pan and simmer gently for ½ hour to 1 hour until meat is tender. Time depends on cut of meat used.
4. Add cilantro and cook for 10 more minutes.

Basic Ground Beef Meat Sauce

This is the base for many dishes such as spaghetti, aushak, mantu, and aush, or vegetables such as peas can be added to it to make a regular quarma. This can be prepared ahead of time and put in the freezer for future use.

1 Large Onion
1 lb. of ground beef
5-6 tablespoons of vegetable oil
2 tablespoons of tomato paste
1 teaspoon coriander
1 teaspoon turmeric
Salt
Pepper
½ teaspoon ginger
1 to 2 cloves of garlic (minced)
1 cup of water

1. In a sauce pan, sauté onion in the oil until transparent.
2. Add the beef and stir until browned.

3. Add tomato paste, coriander, turmeric, salt, pepper, and ginger along with ½ cup of water. Mix well and cook on low to medium heat.

Kachaloo Quarma (Potato Stew with beef)

¼ cup of oil
1 medium onion
3 medium potatoes
½ pound of beef
2 cloves of garlic (minced)
2 jalapeno peppers
1 teaspoon of turmeric
½ cup of tomato puree
½ teaspoon of ginger
Black pepper
Salt
½ cup of washed and chopped cilantro
1 teaspoon of Coriander
4 cups of water

1. Wash beef and cut into small chunks.
2. Slice onions and sauté in oil in a medium pot until it is golden brown.
3. Add meat and stir with onions for 5 minutes.
4. Add garlic, pepper, turmeric, coriander, ginger, salt, and pepper along with jalapeno peppers. Add water and bring to a boil. Cook for 20 minutes.
5. Peel potatoes and cut in medium sized chunks. Add potatoes and tomato puree and stir. Add cilantro and cook for 10-15 minutes on medium heat.
6. Serve with Chalau.

Kachaloo Quarma (Vegetarian)

¼ cup of oil
2 large potatoes
1 onion
2 cloves of garlic (minced)
1 cup of water
¼ cup of tomato puree
1 fresh jalapeno pepper
salt
pepper
½ teaspoon of ginger
1 teaspoon Coriander
1 teaspoon Turmeric
½ cup chopped cilantro (optional)

1. Slice onion and sauté in oil.
2. Peel and cut potato in medium size chunks and sauté with onions for 5 minutes.
3. Add one cup of water along with tomato puree, minced garlic, salt, pepper, ginger, turmeric, coriander, and fresh jalapeno pepper. Add cilantro (optional).
4. Cover pot and let cook for 10-15 minutes or until cooked.
5. Serve with Chalau.

Kohfta (Meatballs)

When I used to eat meat, this was one of my favorite dishes. I have watched my mom make this on several occasions and it always smells and looks so good when she's done. This dish is much easier to cook with a pressure cooker than without.

1 pound ground beef

½ of a cup of oil
4 large Onion
2-3 tablespoons of tomato paste
¼ cup of dal nakhud (split peas)-washed and soaked in advance
6-7 cloves of garlic (minced)
10-15 Alou Bukhara
1 teaspoon black pepper
1-2 teaspoons salt
2 fresh jalapeno pepper
1 teaspoon of turmeric
1 teaspoon of ground ginger
1teaspoon of Coriander
1 egg
water

1. Finely chop 2 onions and set aside.
2. In a large bowl mix the ground beef, onions, 3-4 cloves of minced garlic, egg, ½ teaspoon of black pepper, coriander, ginger, turmeric, salt.
3. Knead the mixture really well with your hands.
4. Make tight ping-pong size balls with your hands and set on a plate.
5. In a pressure cooker, add 8 cups of water and put meatballs in the pressure cooker (do not fasten lid) and bring to a boil for 5 minutes. Remove the meatballs from water and set aside. Do not jam all the meatballs in the pressure cooker. Cook a few at a time for 5 minutes each.
6. Once all the meatballs are removed from the water, put all the meatballs in a colander and rinse with cold water (this is an optional step but it does remove extra fat and impurities from the meatballs).
7. Slice 2 onions and put in a clean pressure cooker with ½ cup of oil. Caramelize on medium heat.
8. Once onions are caramelized, add the meatballs with 3-4 cups of water. Add ½ teaspoon of additional turmeric, coriander, ginger,

salt, pepper, and the remainder of garlic. Fasten the pressure cooker lid and pressure cook for 10 minutes.

9. Add dal nakhud, alou bukhara (if available), and tomato paste along with jalapeno peppers. Stir in and cook on low for an additional 10-15 minutes. Serve with Chalau.

- To cook without pressure cooker, follow to step 8 but cook for an hour prior to moving on to step 9. Also make sure the meatballs have room to move in the pot. If they are squished, they will fall apart. If you have too many meatballs, equally divide the ingredients and use two different pots.
- The Dal Nakhud sticks to the bottom rather quickly, so add it towards the end to the meatballs. You can cook the dal nakhud separately, and then add to the meatball quarma towards the end as well.
- To make Curry meatballs add Quarma Curry recipe to the meatball recipe.

Quarma Gousht (Beef or Lamb)

1 pound of Beef or Lamb
½ cup of oil
2 medium onions
Salt
Black pepper
2 jalapeno peppers
1 teaspoon of Turmeric
½ cup of tomato puree
½ teaspoon of ground ginger
2 cloves of garlic (minced)
1 teaspoon of Coriander
4 cups of water

1. Wash beef thoroughly and cut in small chunks.

2. Slice onions and sauté in oil in a medium pot until golden brown.
3. Add meat and stir with onions for 5 minutes.
4. Add garlic, pepper, turmeric, coriander, ginger, and salt.
5. Add water and bring to a boil. Throw in whole jalapeno peppers and cook for 20 minutes and then add tomato puree after meat is cooked and tender.
6. Can add choice of vegetables such as potato, cauliflower, carrots, green beans, okra, turnips, eggplants, etc. at this point (Wash vegetables and cut in small to medium chunks and add to quarma) and cook for 10 more minutes and serve with Chalau.

- For vegetarian dishes, follow the above recipe minus the meat.

Quarma Lubia Khushk (Dry Bean Stew)

1 pound of Beef or Lamb
1 cup of dry kidney or black eye beans
½ cup of oil
2 medium onions
Salt
Black pepper
2 jalapeno peppers
1 teaspoon of Turmeric
½ cup of tomato puree
½ teaspoon of ground ginger
2 cloves of garlic (minced)
1 teaspoon of Coriander
½ teaspoon of baking soda (optional)
4 cups of water

1. Soak beans for 2-3 hours and then boil until it's cooked.

2. Can use baking soda to speed up the cooking process if a pressure cooker is not used (Can use canned beans and add to quarma after meat is cooked).
3. Cook quarma (follow the recipe for quarma beef) and add beans. Throw in whole jalapeno peppers and cook for 10 minutes.
4. Serve with Chalau.

Khurshaid's Quarma Lubia (Kidney Bean Stew)

This is my aunt's favorite dish and her creation. It tastes great with Chalau.

1 can of red kidney beans
¼ onion (finely chopped)
2-3 tablespoons of oil
1 cup water
1 teaspoon coriander
Salt
Ground red chili pepper to taste
½ teaspoon turmeric
3-4 cloves of minced garlic
¼ teaspoon ground cumin
1-2 tablespoons tomato sauce
Crushed dried mint (optional)

1. Drain and rinse kidney beans and set aside.
2. In a saucepan, sauté onion in oil for about 1-2 minutes or until transparent.
3. Add beans, water, coriander, salt, pepper, turmeric, garlic, cumin, and tomato sauce. Stir and cook on medium heat for about 20-30 minutes.
4. Once ready, add dried mint (optional but tastes good with it) and serve with Chalau.

Quarma Samaruq (Mushroom)

1 cup of mushrooms
½ pound of beef
½ cup of oil
2 medium onions
Salt
Black pepper
2 jalapeno peppers
1 teaspoon of Turmeric
½ cup of tomato puree
½ teaspoon of ground ginger
2 cloves of garlic (minced)
1 teaspoon of Coriander
4 cups of water

1. Wash beef thoroughly and cut in small chunks.
2. Slice onions and sauté in oil in a medium pot until golden brown.
3. Add meat and mushrooms and stir with onions for 5 minutes.
4. Add garlic, pepper, turmeric, coriander, ginger, salt, and pepper. Add water and bring to a boil. Throw in whole jalapeno peppers and cook.
5. Cook for 20 minutes and then add tomato puree after meat is cooked and tender. Serve with white basmati rice.

- For vegetarian dishes, follow the above recipe minus the meat.

Quarma Dal Nakhud and Alou bukhara (splitpeas and plums)

¼ of a cup of Dal Nakhud (split peas)
6-7 Alou Bukhara (Bukhara plums)
½ pound of beef
½ cup of oil

2 medium onions
Salt
Black pepper
2 jalapeno peppers
1 teaspoon of Turmeric
½ cup of tomato puree
½ teaspoon of ground ginger
2 cloves of garlic
1 teaspoon of Coriander
4 cups of water

1. Wash beef thoroughly and cut in small chunks.
2. Slice onions and sauté in oil in a medium pot until golden brown.
3. Add meat and stir with onions for 5 minutes.
4. Add garlic, pepper, turmeric, coriander, ginger, salt, and pepper. Add water and bring to a boil. Cook for 20 minutes and then add tomato puree after meat is cooked and tender.
5. Add plums and dal nakhud and cook for 10 more minutes and serve with white basmati rice.

• For vegetarian dishes, follow the above recipe minus the meat.

Curry Quarma

½ pound of beef or lamb
½ cup of oil
2 medium onions
Salt
Black pepper
2 jalapeno pepper
1 teaspoon of Turmeric
½ cup of tomato puree
1 tablespoon of curry powder
2 tablespoon of white flour
½ teaspoon of ground ginger
2 cloves of garlic (minced)

1 teaspoon of Coriander
4 cups of water

1. Wash meat thoroughly and cut in small chunks.
2. Slice onions and sauté in oil in a medium pot until golden brown.
3. Add meat and stir with onions for 5 minutes.
4. Add tomato puree with a cup of water and boil for 5 minutes and stir occasionally.
5. Add garlic, pepper, turmeric, coriander, ginger, salt, and pepper.
6. Add more water until meat is tender.
7. Add ½ cup of water to curry powder and flour and mix prior to putting it in pot. Once mixed add to meat and onions.
8. Throw in whole jalapeno peppers and cook for 10 minutes and serve with white basmati rice.

• For vegetarian dishes, follow the above recipe minus the meat.

Cherry Quarma

½ pound of beef or lamb
½ cup of oil
1 pound fresh pitted cherries
2 tablespoons of sugar
2 medium onions
Salt
2 jalapeno peppers
½ teaspoon of chili powder
1-2 cardamom seeds (whole)
½ teaspoon of ground ginger
4 cups of water

1. Wash beef thoroughly and cut in small chunks.
2. Slice onions and sauté in oil in a medium pot until golden brown.
3. Add meat and stir with onions for 5 minutes.

4. Add half a cup of water and boil for 3-4 minutes then add the rest of the water until meat is cooked.
5. Add cherries and ginger, salt, sugar, cardamom seeds, and chili powder . Throw in whole jalapeno peppers and cook for 10 more minutes or until cooked. Serve with white basmati rice.

• For vegetarian dishes, follow the above recipe minus the meat.

<u>Quarma Mahi (Fish)</u>

1 pound fish fillets (Mahi Mahi type of fish)
1 cup of oil
2 medium onions
½ teaspoon of red chili powder
salt
Pepper
1 teaspoon Coriander
½ cup of tomato puree
3 cloves of garlic (minced)
½ teaspoon of ground ginger
1 teaspoon of turmeric

1. Wash and cut fish in 3"x3" squares.
2. In a frying pan add oil and fry fish.
3. Take fish out of oil and drain oil from fish.
4. In a pot add ½ cup of oil with sliced onions and stir until golden.
5. Add tomato puree and stir for 5 minutes.
6. Add two cups of water and add fish. Add spices. Cook for 10-15 minutes on low and serve with white basmati rice or plain bread.

Quarma Seb taza (Fresh Apples)

2-3 large apples
¼ pound of beef
½ cup of oil
2 medium onions
Salt
Black pepper
2 jalapeno peppers
1 teaspoon of Turmeric
½ cup of tomato puree
½ teaspoon of ground ginger
1 teaspoon of Coriander
4 cups of water

1. Wash meat thoroughly and cut into small chunks.
2. Slice onions and sauté in oil in a medium pot until it is golden brown.
3. Add meat and stir with onions for 5 minutes.
4. Add minced garlic, pepper, turmeric, coriander, ginger, salt, and pepper.
5. Add water and bring to a boil. Cook for 20 minutes.
6. Cut and peal apples into quarters and add along with tomato puree and stir. Throw in whole jalapeno peppers and cook for 10 minutes and serve with white basmati rice.

Quarma Bamia (Okra)

¼ cup of oil
½ pound of Okra
½ onion (diced)
¼ pound of beef (optional)

2 cloves of garlic (minced)
1 cup of water
¼ cup of tomato puree
1 fresh jalapeno pepper
salt
pepper
½ teaspoon of ground ginger
1 teaspoon Coriander
4 cups of water

1. Wash Okra and cut the ends.
2. Lay cut okra out in sun on a paper towel for 5-10 minutes until dry.
3. Slice onions and sauté in oil in a medium pot until it is golden brown.
4. Optional: Add meat and stir with onions for 5 minutes.
5. Add minced garlic, pepper, turmeric, coriander, ginger, salt, and pepper.
6. Add water and bring to a boil. Cook for 20 minutes.
7. Add Okra along with tomato puree and stir. Throw in jalapeno pepper and cook for 10 minutes.
8. Serve with Chalau.

Quarma Gul-e-Karam (Cauliflower)

½ pound of Cauliflower
¼ cup of split peas
½ teaspoon of fresh Ginger (optional)
plus ingredients for Quarma Gousht

1. Follow recipe for Quarma Gousht and cook for 20 minutes.
2. Separate Cauliflower crowns and wash. Add to Quarma along with ½ cup of water, split peas, and fresh ginger (optional) and cook for 10-15 minutes.

Quarma Shalghum (Turnips)

1 pound of Turnips
½ teaspoon of ginger
¼ cup of tomato puree (less tomato puree than regular quarma's)
3 tablespoons of table sugar
plus ingredients of Quarma Gousht

1. Follow recipe for Quarma Gousht and cook for 20 minutes (for vegetarian dishes cook for 5-10 minutes and then add turnips).
2. Wash and peel turnips. Cut turnips in quarters and add to quarma along with fresh grated ginger, fresh jalapeno pepper, and sugar.
3. Cook for 15-20 minutes or until turnip is cooked.
4. Serve with Chalau.

Quarma Zardak (Carrots)

1 pound carrots
2 tablespoons of table sugar
plus ingredients of Quarma Gousht

1. Follow recipe for Quarma Gousht and cook for 20 minutes.
2. Peel, cut and slice carrots and add to quarma along with sugar and cook for 20 minutes.
3. Serve with Chalau.

Quarma Banjan Rumi (Tomatoes)

¼ pound beef
1 ½ pound of Tomatoes
¼ cup of oil
1 big onion

¼ of split peas
2 cloves of garlic (minced)
2 fresh jalapeno peppers
1 teaspoon of fresh grated ginger
Salt
Pepper
1 teaspoon of coriander
½ teaspoon of turmeric
4 cups of water

1. Wash beef thoroughly and cut in small chunks.
2. Slice onions and sauté in oil in a medium pot until golden brown.
3. Add meat and stir with onions for 5 minutes.
4. Add water and bring to a boil. Cook for 20 minutes.
5. In a separate pot, boil tomatoes for 5 minutes until skin is separated.
6. Let cool and peel skin off tomatoes. Cut in quarters and place in quarma.
7. Add minced garlic, split peas, jalapeno pepper, turmeric, coriander, ginger, salt, pepper and cook for 10-15 minutes.
8. Serve with Chalau.

Quarma Fasilya (Green Bean)

1 pound of Green beans
Ingredients for Quarma Gousht

1. Wash green beans and cut the ends.
2. Follow recipe for Quarma gousht.
3. Cut in half and toss into Quarma gousht after it has been cooking for 20 minutes.
4. Cook green beans 10-15 minutes.
5. Serve with Chalau.

Quarma BanJan (Egg Plant)

1 Eggplant
Ingredients for Quarma Gousht

1. Make quarma gousht.
2. Peel eggplant and cut in chunks, and toss into quarma gousht after it has been cooking for 20 minutes.
3. Cook eggplant 10-15 minutes.
4. Serve with Chalau.

Quarma Sabzee (Spinach)

1 package of frozen spinach or 2 cups fresh chopped Spinach
1 ½ lb. Beef or lamb meat
½ onion (finely chopped)
1 tablespoon of Holba
1 teaspoon Coriander
½ cup chopped Gundana (or leeks)
½ cup chopped cilantro
1 jalapeno pepper
¼ cup black eye peas
2-3 cloves of minced garlic
½ teaspoon ground ginger
Salt and pepper to taste
1-1 ½ cup of water
¼ cup of oil

1. Cut meat into ¾ inch cubes.
2. In a sauce pan, heat oil and fry onion on medium heat until slightly browned.

3. Increase heat to medium high and add meat and garlic. Stir often until meat begins to brown.
4. Add water, salt and pepper to taste. Cook for 10 minutes.
5. Lower heat and add spinach, cilantro, gundana, and black eye peas along with coriander, jalapeno pepper, holba, and ginger. Stir.
6. Cook on medium low further for 10 minutes.
7. Serve with Chalau.

Fish

.Although Afghans do eat fish, it's not a common dish. Afghans usually prepare fish as either kabobs, fried, or as a quarma. The recipes below are not Afghan recipes but I've added these favorite recipes for variety.

Salmon

I accidentally created this recipe and it has become a family favorite ever since, almost to the point of overdose. My non-Afghan friends have also "borrowed" the recipe and have been making this dish and have made the recipe " their own".

3-4 fillets of skinless salmon
4-5 cloves of garlic (minced)
1-2 tablespoons of olive oil (or plain vegetable oil)
Juice of 1 lemon
Salt
Fresh ground black pepper
Italian seasoning mix
2-3 tablespoons of plain yoghurt (optional)

1. Wash salmon and dry with a paper towel. Place in a deep dish and add lemon juice, garlic, salt, pepper, Italian seasoning mix, and yoghurt (optional). Mix salmon in marinade well and cover. Marinade for at least ½ hour in the fridge. The longer the better.
2. In a skillet, add 1-2 tablespoons of olive oil and heat. Add the fish along with the marinade, cover and cook on low heat. If fish begins to burn before cooking, add a ¼ cup of water and cover. Continue to cook over low heat until done. When salmon turns pink inside and out, it is cooked.

•   For variety, you can add onions in skillet (sauté until soft and then add salmon), and then add chopped tomatoes on top of salmon and cook. You can also take the salmon and bake in the deep dish in 350 degree oven for 20-30 minutes. Cover dish with foil prior to putting in oven.

- My favorite way to eat this dish is with brown rice and steamed vegetables. It's also good with basmati rice.

Garlicky Fish Skewers

This recipe is a great alternative to hamburgers at a BBQ.

1 each of small fresh or canned hot red, green, red chilies.
2 large Tomatoes, peeled and diced
1 medium onion, finely chopped
Juice of 1 lemon
¼ teaspoon of salt
1 teaspoon of sugar
1 tablespoon red wine vinegar
3 tablespoons olive oil
3-4 cloves of garlic minced
¼ teaspoon pepper
2 lbs. Firm textured fish steaks (swordfish, halibut, turbot, ling cod) cut into 1-1 ½ inch chunks
Salt

1. Stem, seed, and finely chop chilies. Place chilies in a non reactive bowl and add Tomatoes, onion, salt, sugar, and vinegar. Stir until well blended. Cover and refrigerate for at least 30 minutes or until the next day.
2. In a bowl, combine oil, garlic, lemon juice, and pepper. Add fish chunks and turn to coat. Thread fish chunks equally on 6 sturdy metal skewers.
3. Place foil on the grill and then place the skewers on the foil 4-6 inches above a solid bed of hot coals. Poke holes in the foil and cook turning several times, until fish flakes when prodded in the

thickest part (10-12 minutes). Season to taste with salt and top with relish.

Fish baked with Tomatoes and Garlic

My family absolutely loves this recipe. Prior to this recipe, the only way my family would cook fish was to fry it. Baking fish was a new concept in my family at the introduction of this recipe. We ate this dish to the point of over-dose as well.

2 lbs. Cod, halibut, Mahi-Mahi, or haddock fillets or steaks
Salt
Juice of 2 lemons
2 sliced onions
2-3 cloves garlic, minced
½ cup olive oil
4 chopped Tomatoes
½ cup chopped parsley (thoroughly washed, then chopped)
1 teaspoon paprika
½ teaspoon sugar
2 bay leaves (optional)

1. Wash the fish and drain it. Sprinkle it with a little salt and juice of 1 lemon. Set it aside for 30 minutes.
2. Sauté the onions and garlic lightly in ¼ cup of olive oil. Add the Tomatoes and parsley and continue cooking for 2-3 minutes. Stir in the bay leaves, paprika, salt, and sugar, and set aside.
3. Butter a baking dish and arrange half the sautéed vegetables on the bottom. Arrange the fish on top of the vegetables. Spread the remaining vegetables over the fish. Combine the ¼ cup of olive oil, and lemon juice, and pour over all. Bake, covered, at 350° F for 30 minutes. Uncover and continue baking 10 more minutes, or until the fish is done.

Mantu, and Aushak

Mantu

This is a popular dish in Afghanistan. Mantu is best described as steamed meat dumpling, similar to Tibetan and Chinese dishes. This dish can be made from scratch or with pasta wraps. If you want to make from scratch, follow the dough recipe for Aushak below.

1 package of Azumaya Pasta Wraps (small squares)
1 lb. Ground Beef
1 Onion
1 bunch of Cilantro
½ teaspoon of ground red chili peppers
½ teaspoon ground black pepper
1 teaspoon coriander
3-4 cloves of minced garlic
2 cups of water

Yogurt mix
1 cup of yogurt
2-3 cloves of garlic
dried mint

1. In a food processor, chop onion and cilantro coarsely.
2. In a pot, add cilantro, onion, and ground beef along with spices and 2 cups of water. Cook for 8-10 minutes on medium heat.
3. Take pasta wraps and fill them with a small amount of the meat mixture, wet the edges and close, making little triangles.
4. Brush pasta wraps with a little bit of oil on both sides and set aside until all are filled.
5. In a steam pot, add water on the bottom and grease the steamer with a little bit of oil (this is to prevent the mantu from sticking).

6. Cover the pot with a lid and allow to cook on medium high heat for about 45 minutes. Check pot occasionally for proper water level for steaming.
7. Prepare sauce base and set aside.
8. Smear yogurt mix on the bottom of a platter.
9. Gently remove the mantu from the steamer and lay on top of the yogurt in the platter.
10. Add sauce base on top of mantu and cover with more yogurt mix. Sprinkle red pepper if desired, along with dried mint. Serve.

Sauce Base
1 Medium Onion
¼ lb. of ground beef
5-6 tablespoons of vegetable oil
2 tablespoons of tomato paste
1 teaspoon Coriander
1 teaspoon Turmeric
Salt
Pepper
½ Teaspoon Ginger
1-2 cloves of Garlic (minced)
¼ cup dal nakhud (pre-washed and soaked)
1 cup of water

1. In a sauce pan, sauté onion in the oil until transparent.
2. Add the beef and stir until browned.
3. Add tomato paste, coriander, turmeric, salt, pepper, dal nakhud and ginger along with ½ cup of water. Mix well and cook on low to medium heat.

Aushuk

This dish is similar to raviolis but filled with leeks and topped with ground beef and yogurt. I made it from scratch with my father one time and it proved to be very time consuming. Using the pasta wraps sold at stores saves a lot of time.

Dough Mix:
1 cup all purpose flour
1 egg
1 tablespoons of vegetable oil
1 tablespoons of salt

Azumaya Pasta Wrappers (small round package):
1 cup of chopped Gundana (or Chives/leeks)
½ lb. of Ground Beef
½ Onion, sliced
3-4 tablespoons of oil
1-2 tablespoons of Tomato Paste
1 teaspoon of Coriander
½ teaspoon of Turmeric
½ teaspoon of Ginger
1 teaspoon dried crushed red peppers
Salt
Pepper
2-3 cloves of Garlic (minced)
Water
1 cup plain yogurt or quroot
Dried mint (crushed)

Meat Sauce: To be prepared ahead of time.
1. In a sauce pan, sauté onion in the oil until transparent.
2. Add the beef and stir until browned.
3. Add tomato paste, coriander, turmeric, salt, pepper, and ginger along with ½ cup of water. Mix well and cook on low to medium heat.

4. Keep warm and set aside

Noodle

Won Ton pasta wraps:
1. Thoroughly wash Gundana and chop finely.
2. Add salt and crushed red peppers to the Gundana and mix well. Set aside.
3. Chinese won-ton wrappers: Take one wrapper out of package, and wet the outer edges with water.
4. Place a small amount of chopped Gundana in the center and close the wrapper, making a triangle. Keep doing this until all the Gundana is finished.
5. In a large pot, add 2 quarts of water and bring to a boil.
6. Add finished won-ton triangles to the boiling water and boil for about 8-10 minutes.
7. Gently remove the won tons out of the water, drain, and set aside.
8. In a bowl, mix the yogurt and garlic.
9. In a large platter, smear 2 tablespoons of yogurt mix on the platter and put the won tons on top of the yogurt.
10. Put the meat sauce on the won tons.
11. Put 4-5 tablespoons of yogurt on top of the entire platter.
12. Sprinkle mint over yogurt and meat sauce and serve.

Dough rounds:
1. Add 1 tablespoons of salt to the all-purpose flour and sift.
2. Add the egg and oil and mix well.
3. Add ½ cup of water slowly and knead the dough real well. Knead until dough becomes smooth.
4. Divide dough in to 2-3 balls, set aside and cover for about an hour.
5. Once dough has risen, take a small chunk out of the balls, make a small ball out of it and roll out on a floured board with a rolling pin. Roll out to a thin round circle.

6. Use a round cutter about 2-3 inches in diameter to cut out rounds. Repeat until dough is finished. Flour rounds and don't place directly on top of each other so they don't stick together.
7. Using the water from the Gundana, or regular water, wet one side of the rounds, on the edge.
8. Take a small amount of Gundana and place in the center of the rounds. Bring edges of rounds together and seal carefully. Set aside until all are done.
9. Follow steps 5-12 from above.

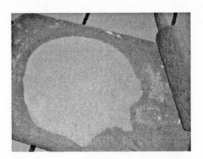

Roll out dough

Cut out a dough round with a cutter

Cut out dough round from center and set aside

Shell Pasta with Yogurt sauce

This is one American favorite that has been "Afghanized". My mom popularized this dish by adding Afghan spices to the dish and steaming it along with adding yogurt and gundana for added flavor. This has been a hit at several dinner parties.

1 package of large shell pasta
Recipe for Basic Ground Beef Meat Sauce
1 cup of yogurt
Dried crushed mint
½ cup chopped Gundana (or leeks)
½ can of red kidney beans

1. Follow recipe for basic ground beef meat sauce. Set aside.
2. Boil pasta shells in water until al dente (not too soft).
3. Drain pasta and put in a deep dish pot with a lid.
4. Add beans to ground beef sauce and mix.
5. Take out a cup of beef sauce and mix with pasta in pot. Add ¼ cup of water. Mix well with pasta.
6. Cover the lid with a clean cloth and place on pot.
7. Steam the pasta on medium low heat for about 10-15 minutes.
8. Remove pasta and place on a platter.
9. Add an additional cup of ground beef sauce over the pasta.
10. Sprinkle chopped gundana over the meat sauce and pasta.
11. Add ½ cup of yogurt over the gundana and sprinkle with mint. Serve with additional meat sauce and yogurt separately to be added per individual taste.

Soups
(Aush, Maushawa, etc.)

Aush (Soup)-with meat

1 package of eggnoodles (Fresh Chinese noodles preferred)
2 quarts of water
½ pound ground beef
¼ cup of oil
1 onion
¾ cup of tomato puree
3 cloves of garlic (minced)
½ teaspoon of ground ginger
½ teaspoon of coriander
3 cups of yoghurt or Quroot
2 tablespoons of split peas
½ cup of kidney beans
½ cup of chick-peas
Salt
Pepper
1 tablespoons of crushed mint

1. Slice onions and sauté in oil until golden brown.
2. Add ground beef and stir with onions and oil for 5 minutes.
3. Add tomato puree, salt, pepper, 2 cloves of garlic, ginger, and coriander, along with 1 cup of water and let boil for 20 minutes.
4. In a separate pot, add 2 quarts of water, the noodles and a pinch of salt and bring to a boil. Let boil for 10-15 minutes.
5. Drain noodles. Take noodles and put in big bowel and mix with the beef.
6. In a bowel, mix 1 clove of garlic to the yoghurt and set aside.
7. Add yogurt to noodles and mix.
8. Sprinkle mint and serve.

Aush (Soup)-Vegetarian

½ package of egg-noodles (Fresh Chinese noodles preferred)
2 quarts of water
¼ cup of oil
1 onion
¼ cup of tomato sauce
2 clove of garlic (minced)
3 cups of plain yoghurt
1can of kidney beans (rinse)
1 can of Garbanzo beans (rinse)
1-2 potatoes
Salt (to taste)
Pepper (to taste)
1 teaspoon coriander
1 teaspoon turmeric
1 teaspoon ground ginger
1 tablespoons of crushed dry mint

1. In a deep pot, slice onions and sauté in oil until golden brown.
2. Cut potato in quarters and add to onions with 2 cups of water and boil for 5-7 minutes.
3. Add noodles, tomato puree, salt, kidney beans, garbanzo beans, pepper, minced garlic, coriander, turmeric, and ginger, along with 5-6 cups of water and let boil for 20 minutes.
4. Once it's ready (noodles tender, and water soupy) take Ash out and place in a bowl and add yoghurt and mix.
5. Sprinkle dry mint over the Ash and serve.

Malalai's Aush Recipe

This recipe was kindly shared with me by my cousin Malalai. I wanted to include this recipe in the book because it's also a favorite variation of the Aush recipe of mine. Malalai has made this dish for me on several occasions, especially when at a particular dinner party she knew there would be mostly meat dishes and I'd have nothing to eat. I'm grateful for her thoughtfulness and for this recipe.

1 package of Fresh Chinese Noodles
3 Potatoes
1 can of garbanzo beans
1 ½ can of kidney beans
1-2 cups of yogurt
3-4 quarts of water
1 cup tomato sauce
2 cloves of minced garlic
1 teaspoon of coriander
½ teaspoon turmeric
½ teaspoon black pepper
Salt
3 tablespoons of oil
Dried mint
Red pepper (ground or crushed)

1. In a deep pot add water, noodles, and 2-3 tablespoons of salt. Allow to cook for 20-30 minutes on medium high heat.
2. In a colander, rinse the kidney and garbanzo beans. Separate half a can of Kidney beans and set aside.
3. Add kidney beans and garbanzo beans to the noodles and mix. Cook for an additional 1-2 minutes.
4. When done, put Aush in a deep serving bowl and mix in yogurt.
5. Make sauce in a saucepan by adding tomato sauce, garlic, coriander, turmeric, pepper, 1 teaspoon of salt, ½ can of kidney beans, and 3 tablespoons of oil. Simmer for 10 minutes on medium low heat.
6. Add sauce to the Aush and mix.
7. Sprinkle mint and pepper as desired and serve in bowls.

Vegetarian Vegetable Soup

½ Onion (chopped)
¼ cup of oil
¼ cup of 7 bean mix (dry)
2 potatoes (cut in quarters)
1 cup of frozen mixed "Fiesta" Vegetable mix
¼ cup of frozen green peas
3-4 cloves of garlic (minced)
2-3 tablespoons of tomato puree
10-15 spaghetti noodles (broken into 4 quarters)
1 teaspoon coriander
Salt
Pepper
1 lemon or lime
Water

1. In a deep pot, add the oil and onion and fry for about 3 minutes. Add 4-5 cups of water along with bean mix and cook for 10-15 minutes.
2. Add potatoes along with 3-4 cups of water and bring to a boil with the lid on for about 8-10 minutes.
3. Add about 2-3 quarts of water along with the mixed vegetables, peas, noodles, tomato puree, garlic, salt, pepper, and coriander. Allow to cook on medium heat for about 15-20 minutes.
4. Once ready, put in bowls and serve with lemon and bread. The lemon makes it more flavorful.

- This is my own personal recipe that I created when I used to get sick. Because of the onion and the garlic in the soup, I always used to feel that it would cure whatever I might've had. It usually made me feel better and was also perfect for those cold winter nights.
- The 7-bean mix is commonly found in bulk in most health food stores. Beans should be washed and soaked ahead of time, preferably over an hour.

Maushawa (Bean and Meatball Soup)

½ cup dried red kidney beans, washed and soaked overnight
Water
½ cup yellow split peas
½ cup mung beans
½ cup short grain rice
salt
½ cup oil
1 large onion
water
½ cup chopped tomatoes
1 teaspoon dill (shibit)-dry or fresh
1 cup yoghurt

Meatballs:
8 oz. Finely ground beef or lamb
½ teaspoon salt
½ teaspoon freshly ground black pepper
¼ teaspoon hot chili pepper
¼ teaspoon ground cinnamon

1. Drain beans and place in a large pot, add 2-3 cups of water and bring to a boil. Cover and simmer on medium heat for about an hour.
2. Wash split peas and mung beans and add to pot with 2 more cups of water. Allow to simmer for an additional 30 minutes.
3. Wash rice and add to pot with 2 teaspoons salt. Simmer for another 30 minutes until the ingredients are soft.
4. Combine ground meat with seasonings and shape into small round balls (meatball size).
5. Heat oil in a large skillet and fry onion until transparent and lightly browned. Add meatballs and fry, stirring often, until browned. Stir in water and tomatoes, cover and simmer for 30 minutes. This can be done simultaneously while beans are

cooking. Add cooked bean mixture, another 2 cups of water, and dill. Bring to a boil and then add yoghurt, stirring over low heat until almost boiling. Adjust seasoning with salt and more chili pepper if desired. Serve hot in bowls with bread. Sprinkle dried mint over bowls if desired.

Chicken or Beef soup

Half a chicken or one pound of beef or lamb
¼ of cup of split peas
1 onion
Salt
3 whole Cardamom
½ a bunch of Cilantro
Black pepper
3-4 quarts of water

1. Wash meat clean and place in a deep pot and add water.
2. Boil the meat in water and collect the foam from the water.
3. Cut onion in rings and add to water with split peas, salt to taste and cardamom.
4. Boil the mixture until cooked.
5. Add water if needed while meat is cooking.
6. Add cilantro to cooked meat and boil for 1-2 minutes.
7. Add black pepper and serve with fresh vegetables, lemon and bread.

• Can put in bowl and be eaten with a spoon or with bread and vegetables.

Bean Soup

1 pound of Chicken, beef, or lamb
¼ cup of vegetable oil
½ pound of Tomatoes (two small Tomatoes)
Salt
Pepper
1 teaspoon of turmeric
2-3 Quarts of water
¼ cup of dry red beans
¼ cup of split peas
1 ½ pound of potatoes (2-3 large potatoes)
1 tablespoons of Coriander
1 small onion
Fresh cilantro

1. Wash meat thoroughly and cut into chunks.
2. Cut onion in rings and sauté in oil until onion is golden brown.
3. Add meat to sautéed onion and stir onion, oil and meat together.
4. Cut Tomatoes in small chunks and add to meat and stir.
5. Add salt and pepper to taste, turmeric, red bean, split peas and coriander to meat.
6. Add water. Boil meat until it is tender.
7. Add Potatoes and boil with meat until meat and potatoes are both cooked.
8. Add fresh cilantro and cook for 2-3 minutes and serve.

Non-Afghan Favorite Soup Recipes

Potato Lemon Soup (Batata Ben Lamoun)

This recipe was given to me by my friend Nicole Frank, who lives in Humboldt County along with her husband and children. I used to go to her house for Friday Sabbath dinners while I was a "big sister" to her daughter Shira, and she'd make this dish. I fell in love with it and asked her for the recipe. I made the soup on my own and it was delicious.

6-8 stalks of celery
4-5 carrots
Juice of 3-4 lemons
¼ teaspoon turmeric
2-3 tablespoon corn oil (not Mazola, something from health food store, it should be a nice orange color)
6-7 cloves of garlic pressed
12 medium sized potatoes peeled and cut into cubes or slices
several quarts of water
1-2 vegetarian bouillon cubes
salt to taste

1. Fill your soup pot ¾ of the way full with water, place on stove and start the heat.
2. In a food processor grind up the carrots and celery. Add them to the water and let the whole shebang boil vigorously. Skim the scummy stuff off the top and discard.
3. In a small saucepan heat the oil on low and add the garlic, cook until foamy. Don't let the garlic get brown. Add this to the water and celery, turn the heat to medium, let cook for 5-10 minutes.
4. Add potatoes and cook on low to medium for twenty minutes, stirring occasionally.
5. Soup is ready for the other ingredients when you can mush up the potatoes in the soup with a masher. Mash up the potatoes in the soup then add the bouillon cubes, turmeric, lemon juice and a drop of salt. Stir and let cook another five minutes, serve with bread.

Yogurt Soup with Mint

2 quarts beef, chicken, or vegetable stock
½ cup rice
4 eggs yolks
3 cups yogurt
6 tablespoons all-purpose flour
1 ½ cups water
4 tablespoons butter
3-4 tablespoons dried mint leaves, crushed
½ teaspoon or more cayenne or paprika

1. Put the stock and rice in a pan, cover and simmer until the rice is soft, about 30 minutes.
2. In a mixing bowl, beat the egg yolks with yogurt and flour. Add the water and blend to the consistency of a thin batter. Gradually add this to the soup through a sieve, stirring constantly. Cover and simmer 10-15 minutes. Remove from heat.
3. Melt 4 tablespoons of butter in a saucepan, stir in the mint leaves and cayenne or paprika, and cook until bubbly. Gently stir this mixture into the hot soup. Serve immediately.

Red Lentil Soup

1 cup red lentils, picked over and washed several times
2 tablespoons uncooked short-grain rice
2 quarts meat (or vegetable) stock or water
1-2 finely minced onions
4 tablespoons of butter
6 tablespoons all-purpose flour
3 egg yolks
1 cup milk

1. Cook the lentils and rice together in the stock or water until soft, about 45 minutes. Press through a sieve and set aside. Discard the residue remaining in the sieve.
2. Sauté the onions in 4 tablespoons butter in a large saucepan until golden brown. Blend in the flour and stir 2-3 minutes over medium heat. Slowly pour the hot lentil-rice mixture into the onions and flour, stirring briskly with a wire whisk to blend until thick and smooth. Cover and simmer gently 10-15 minutes, stirring occasionally.
3. Beat the egg yolks with the milk and stir into the soup. Bring just to a boil. Remove from heat. The consistency should be that of a cream soup. Hot water may be added if necessary to thin. Sprinkle croutons over individual bowls of hot soup.

Gazpacho (Cold Vegetable soup)

This is a Spanish soup that is very refreshing on hot summer days. I first became familiar with this soup when I went to Spain. While in Granada, Spain, we ate this soup almost everyday for lunch and I just loved it.

1 cup peeled and chopped tomatoes
½ cup finely chopped celery
1 medium cucumber (peeled, seeded, chopped)
1 medium green bell peppers (chopped)
1 medium red bell pepper (chopped)
½ cup green onion (chopped)
½ cup parsley (chopped)
1-2 cloves of garlic (minced)
3 tablespoons red wine vinegar
2 tablespoons olive oil
2 ½ cups of tomato juice
¾ teaspoon salt
Pepper to taste

1. Throw tomatoes in boiling water for 1 minute and then drain. Once cool, peel the skin off and chop tomatoes finely.
2. In a food processor or blender, put all ingredients and pulse, and coarsely chop vegetables.
3. Put in the refrigerator and allow to cool for 1-2 hours. Serve chilled. Garnish with mint and a small amount of chopped vegetables (i.e. tomatoes, cucumbers, and bell peppers)

Kabobs

Chapli Kabob

1 lb. all purpose flour
1 lb. ground beef
1 onion
3-4 cloves of minced garlic
2-3 tablespoons of coriander
½ teaspoon turmeric
½ teaspoon black pepper
2 tablespoons salt
¼ cup fresh cilantro (chopped)
¼ cup of oil

1. In a food processor, chop the onion.
2. In a bowl, mix the beef, flour, onion, garlic, coriander, turmeric, black pepper, salt, and cilantro. Knead mix well.
3. Make the mixture into flat patties (like Hamburgers).
4. In a skillet, add ¼ cup of oil and heat on high. Reduce heat to low and place patties in skillet and slowly cook until patties are done (about 20-30 minutes). Watch patties so they don't dry out.
5. Serve with other kabobs or make a hamburger sandwich out of it.

Shami Kabob (Also known as Lola Kabob)

This recipe belongs to my aunt Aquila. I don't eat meat but on several occasions, I have eaten 1-2 of these at dinner parties because they are so delicious. As a child I used to eat the ground beef mixture before the kabobs were fried because I loved the taste so much. I used to say that if I ever ate meat again, it would be for the lola kabobs. At several dinner parties we have sneaked several of these kabobs prior to serving due to fear that we might not get any once the guests begin to eat.

2 lbs. Beef
3 Potatoes
1 big onion (sliced)
Black Pepper
4-5 cloves of minced garlic
1-2 teaspoons of coriander
½ cup of cilantro
3 eggs (Yolks and Whites separated)
Salt
Water

1. Wash and cut beef into chunks.
2. In a saucepan, add beef with onion, coriander, salt, and turmeric along with 1-2 cups of water.   Cook on medium heat for 30-40 minutes or until well done.
3. Boil potatoes separately until soft. Set aside and let cool.
4. Peel potatoes, and cut in chunks.
5. When meat is cooked, take out and put in a food processor along with potatoes, pepper, garlic, and cilantro. Grind mixture really well.
6. Take out meat mixture and place in a bowl. Add egg yolks and mix with salt and turmeric. Knead mixture with your hands really well.
7. Take a small amount of the mixture and roll with your hands into small rolls, using the eggwhite mixture to stick the meat together.
8. Once all the meat has been used and made into rolls, fry the rolls in 1 cup of oil on medium heat until browned.
9. Serve with rice or bread.

Khurshaid's Chicken Kabob

This is my aunt's specialty. She usually makes it for special "girl's only" dinner parties at her house and it's always a hit with everyone. I made it once for my aunt and cousin Sitara and it was a hit.

2-3 chicken breasts cut into 1-inch cubes
2 lemons
1 teaspoon of coriander
1 teaspoon turmeric
Salt
1 teaspoon of ground red chili pepper
1 teaspoon of ground ginger
4-5 cloves of garlic (minced)
1-2 Green Bell Peppers (cut into small pieces)
2-3 Potatoes (peeled and chopped in small chunks)
2-3 tablespoons of olive oil
2 teaspoons of curry powder
½ cup of chopped cilantro
2-3 cups of water

1. In a deep pot, add chicken and oil, along with juice of 2 lemons, coriander, turmeric, salt, pepper, ginger, garlic, and water, and cook for 5-10 minutes on medium heat (with pot covered).
2. Add the potatoes, mix well and cook for an additional 10-15 minutes. Add more water as needed.
3. Once chicken and potatoes are done, add curry powder, bell peppers, and cilantro and cook for an additional 5-7 minutes.
4. Serve with rice or bread.

Khurshaid's Chicken Kabob

Chicken Kabob

2 ½ -3 lbs. Boned chicken, cut into 1-inch cubes
1/2 cup olive oil
Juice of 2 lemons
3 cloves garlic, mashed
2 teaspoons thyme
1 teaspoon salt
½ teaspoon coarsely ground black pepper
8 cherry Tomatoes
4-8 boiling onions, trimmed whole
1-2 green bell peppers, cut in 1-inch squares

1. Put the chicken cubes in a bowl.

2. Mix together the oil, lemon juice, garlic, thyme, salt, and black pepper.
3. Pour over the chicken and blend well.
4. Refrigerate over night.
5. Thread the chicken on the skewers alternately with the cherry Tomatoes, onions, and green peppers.
6. Grill over a charcoal fire, turning and basting frequently. Be careful not to overcook.

Chicken Kabob

Marinated Chicken Kabob

1 frying chicken
1 cup yogurt
½ grated onion
3-4 cloves of garlic, mashed
Juice of ½ lemon
1 tablespoon ground cumin
1 tablespoon paprika
Salt and pepper

1. Cut the chicken into small pieces.
2. Cut the thighs and legs in half, the breast in similarly sized portions.
3. Mix together the yogurt, onion, garlic, lemon juice, cumin, paprika, salt, and pepper.
4. Put the chicken in a mixing bowl and pour the marinade over it. Mix to coat the chicken pieces well.
5. Refrigerate overnight or 8-10 hours.
6. Grill the chicken over a charcoal fire, turning and basting frequently. Allow 20-25 minutes cooking time.

Lamb Shish Kabob

3 lbs. Boneless lamb shoulder or leg, cut into 1-inch cubes
1 onion, sliced paper thin
1 ½ teaspoon salt
¼ cup olive oil
1 tablespoon vinegar
1 teaspoon coarsely ground pepper
½ teaspoon thyme leaves
2 green bell peppers, cut into 1-inch squares

8-16 pearl onions or quarters of large onions
8-16 cherry Tomatoes

1. Put the meat cubes in a bowl. Put the onions on top and sprinkle salt over them. Squeeze the onions by the handful to press out their juice.
2. Add the olive oil, vinegar, pepper, and thyme; mix thoroughly. Put the pieces of bell pepper on top, cover with wax paper, and refrigerate over night.
3. Remove the meat from the refrigerator 1 hour before cooking. Mix well.
4. Thread the meat on the skewers alternately with the pearl onions or onion chunks, green pepper pieces, and Tomatoes.
5. Broil over charcoal, 3 inches from red-hot coals, turning skewers frequently. If the fire is hot enough, cooking takes 4-6 minutes. Be careful not to overcook or the meat will be dry and flavorless. It should be very juicy and pinkish on the inside. Serve immediately.
6. Serve with rice.

Dolmas

<u>Dolma (Base)</u>

½ pound of ground beef
1 medium onion
4 tablespoons of oil
1 cup of Birinj-e-luk (long grain rice)
2 tablespoons of tomato puree
1 clove of garlic
½ teaspoon of ginger
Salt
Pepper

<u>Sauce</u>
1 medium onion
3-4 tablespoons of oil
1 cup water
1 clove of garlic
½ cup tomato puree
½ teaspoon of turmeric
3-4 fresh jalapeno peppers
Salt (to taste)
Pepper (to taste)

1. Dice onions and sauté in oil until golden brown.
2. Add ground beef and garlic and stir with onions and oil until browned.
3. Add tomato, salt, pepper, and ginger and stir.
4. In a separate pot bring rice to a boil until slightly soft.
5. Drain water and add to the beef pot.

<u>Sauce</u>
1. Dice onions and sauté in oil until golden brown.
2. Add tomato puree, garlic, turmeric, jalapeno peppers and water and let boil for 5 minutes.

Dolma Banjan (Eggplant)

3 medium eggplants
½ pound of ground beef
1 medium onion
4 tablespoons of oil
1 cup of Birinj-e-luk (long grain rice)
2 tablespoons of tomato puree
1 clove of garlic
½ teaspoon of ginger
Salt
Pepper

1. Dice onions and sauté in oil until golden brown.
2. Add ground beef and garlic and stir with onions and oil until browned.
3. Add tomato, salt, pepper, and ginger and stir.
4. In a separate pot bring rice to a boil until slightly soft.
5. Drain water and add to the beef pot.
6. Wash eggplant cut end and put away.
7. Dig out the meat of the eggplant and fill with dolma.
8. Fill all three and put the end back on top of the eggplant.
9. Place eggplants close together in a deep pot.
10. Add sauce over the eggplants and cover pot.
11. Let cook on low for 20-25 minutes.
12. Serve with fresh bread.

Dolma Murch Shireen (Bell Peppers)

3-5 Bell peppers
½ pound of ground beef
1 medium onion
4 tablespoons of oil

1 cup of Birinj-e-luk (long grain rice)
2 tablespoons of tomato puree
1 clove of garlic
½ teaspoon of ginger
Salt
Pepper

1. Dice onions and sauté in oil until golden brown.
2. Add ground beef and garlic and stir with onions and oil until browned.
3. Add tomato, salt, pepper, and ginger and stir.
4. In a separate pot bring rice to a boil until slightly soft.
5. Drain water and add to the beef pot.
6. Wash bell peppers cut end and put away.
7. Dig out the seeds of the peppers and fill with dolma.
8. Fill all and put the end back on top of the peppers.
9. Place peppers close together in a deep pot.
10. Add sauce over the peppers and cover pot.
11. Let cook on low for 20-25 minutes.
12. Serve with fresh bread.

Dolma Banjan Rumi (Tomatoes)

4-5 Large Tomatoes
½ pound of ground beef
1 medium onion
4 tablespoons of oil
1 cup of Birinj-e-luk (long grain rice)
2 tablespoons of tomato puree
1 clove of garlic
½ teaspoon of ginger
Salt
Pepper

1. Dice onions and sauté in oil until golden brown.
2. Add ground beef and garlic and stir with onions and oil until browned.
3. Add tomato, salt, pepper, and ginger and stir.
4. In a separate pot bring rice to a boil until slightly soft.
5. Drain water and add to the beef pot.
6. Wash Tomatoes, cut ends and put away.
7. Dig out the meat of the Tomatoes and fill with dolma.
8. Fill all and put the end back on top of the Tomatoes.
9. Place Tomatoes close together in a deep pot.
10. Add sauce over the Tomatoes and cover pot.
11. Let cook on low for 20-25 minutes.
12. Serve with fresh bread.

Bourani's
(Kachaloo, Banjan, and Kadu)
& Boulani

Kachaloo Bourani (Potatoes)

I think this particular dish has kept me alive during my time of living on my own. I would make this dish at least once a week because it tastes good, was very quick, and easy. For the longest time, this was the only Afghan recipe I was good at making.

4-5 potatoes
3-4 tablespoons of oil
1-2 tablespoons of tomato puree
3 cloves garlic (minced)
½ teaspoon of turmeric
1 cup of yoghurt
¾ cup of water
1 fresh jalapeno pepper
Salt and pepper

1. Peel and slice potatoes thinly (¼ inch).
2. In a frying pan, add oil and 2 cloves of minced garlic.
3. Fry garlic for 1-2 minutes and then add the potatoes.
4. Stir potatoes, garlic and oil for 2-3 minutes and add water, tomato puree, turmeric, salt, pepper, and jalapeno pepper and mix.
5. Cover pan with lid and cook for 8-10 minutes until potatoes are cooked.
6. In a separate bowel add 1 cup of yoghurt and 1 clove of minced garlic and mix.
7. Smear some yogurt on a platter and place potato bourani on the yoghurt. Add more yoghurt on the potatoes and sprinkle some dry mint on top and serve.

Kachaloo Bourani (Potatoes)

Banjan Bourani (Eggplant dish with yoghurt sauce)

This is also one of my favorite dishes. Although it takes time to make, it's well worth it. You can fry all the eggplants in one sitting and put in the freezer for later use. I don't know if other Afghans eat this as much as we do but my mom makes this dish very often and it's a regular at most family gatherings.

3 medium size eggplants
oil for frying
½ cup of water
3-4 cloves of minced garlic
2 Tomatoes (sliced)
Turmeric
1-2 cerrano chilies
1 cup of plain Yoghurt
Dried mint (crushed)
Salt

1. Wash eggplant and cut from top to bottom in rings ½ " thick. Slash (3 times) center of eggplant pieces with a knife and sprinkle with salt. Sprinkle salt liberally on eggplant rings and let sit for 3 hours or so. Dry eggplant with paper towel.
2. In a deep-dish skillet, heat oil (enough for deep frying) and fry eggplant until browned on both sides and set aside.
3. Drain oil out and put eggplant back in skillet with ½ cup of water. Add garlic, a pinch of salt, and 1 teaspoon of turmeric. Place the sliced Tomatoes over eggplant. Add cerrano chilies and cover skillet with lid and cook on medium heat for 10-15 minutes.
4. In a bowl, mix 1 cup of yoghurt with 1 clove of minced garlic.
5. In a platter, smear some of the yoghurt mix on the surface and take out eggplant and Tomatoes gently and place over yoghurt. Pour 3-4 tablespoons of yoghurt mix over entire eggplant. Sprinkle dried mint over the yoghurt and eggplant. Serve with bread and additional yoghurt if desired.

Banjan Bourani (Eggplant dish with yoghurt sauce)

Kudu Bourani (Pumpkin dish with yoghurt sauce)

This is also a very delicious dish. You can usually order this from Afghan restaurants and it's a hit with non-Afghans.

1 squash or pumpkin (cut into thin slices)
1 teaspoon coriander
¾ teaspoon turmeric
Salt
4-5 cloves of minced garlic
1 tablespoon sugar
Black pepper to taste
Oil for frying
1 cup of water
1 cup of yogurt
Dried mint

1. In a deep set skillet add 2-3 cups of oil. Heat on high and then reduce heat to medium setting.
2. Fry the pumpkin until browned and set aside.
3. Empty the oil from skillet and put the pumpkin back in. Add coriander, turmeric, salt, garlic, sugar, and pepper, along with 1 cup of water. Cover the skillet and cook on low for about 20 minutes.
4. In a cup, add yogurt and 1-2 cloves of minced garlic and mix.
5. In a platter, smear some of the yogurt mixture on the bottom.
6. Take Kudu out and place on the platter.
7. Add additional yogurt mix over Kudu, sprinkle with mint and serve with bread.

Boulani Kachaloo (Potatoes)

½ bunch of cilantro (washed thoroughly and chopped)
4-5 green leeks or Gundana (washed thoroughly and chopped)
5-6 potatoes (boiled and peeled)
1 teaspoon crushed red peppers
Salt (to taste)
1 teaspoon Black Pepper
Dough mix (use recipe for Aushak) or Azumaya pasta wraps (large square)
Oil for deep frying

1. Either follow dough mix recipe or use Azumaya pasta wraps.
2. Mash the boiled potatoes either with your hand, a potato masher, or put through the meat grinder to mix.
3. Take potato mix and add cilantro, gundana (or leeks), salt, black pepper, and crushed red peppers. Knead mix well. Check salt level and add more as needed.
4. If using dough, take out a small piece of dough and make into a ball. Then flatten the ball with a rolling pin, sprinkling with flour to prevent sticking. Make the ball very thin and round.
5. Using either the dough or the pasta wraps, take a small amount of the potato mix and place in the middle of the wraps.
6. Dip your fingers in water and wet the edges of the wrap. Fold wrap over and seal edges. Sprinkle flour to prevent sticking and set aside. Follow this process for the remainder of the potato mixture.
7. Once all the wraps have been filled, heat ¼ cup of oil in a deep set skillet. Once oil is hot, turn the heat down to medium low.
8. Place 2-3 filled wraps in the skillet and brown slowly on both sides. Once golden brown, remove from oil, allowing oil to drip back into skillet for a few seconds prior to placing it on the platter. Put a paper towel on the platter to catch the oil. Continue this process until all the wraps have been fried. Add oil to the skillet as needed.
9. Serve hot with Yogurt and Cilantro Chutney mix.

Dal

This is more of an Indian/Pakistani dish but is becoming more popular among Afghans, probably because on our journey out of Afghanistan, most of us spent quiet some time in Pakistan while waiting for our visa's to leave the country and in turn adopted some of their recipes. It's a quick and easy meal to make...perfect for those of us limited on time and/or limited culinary skills.

1 cup of Dal
½ onion (chopped)
2-3 tablespoons of oil
2-3 cups of water
1 teaspoon of turmeric
1 teaspoon of salt
1 teaspoon of coriander
½ teaspoon ground red chili pepper
½ cup chopped cilantro
3-4 cloves of minced garlic
1 lemon

1. In a sauce pan, sauté onion in oil until soft and slightly browned.
2. Add water, dal, turmeric, coriander, salt, chili pepper, garlic and cilantro. Cover pot with lid and cook for about 20-30 minutes on medium heat.
3. Squeeze lemon juice on top and serve with rice or bread.

- For variation, after you cook dal, you can fry 2-3 cloves of minced garlic in a small amount of oil and then add to the dal when it's being served.

Tokhum
(Eggs)

All the egg dishes taste great with green chutney and afghan bread. These dishes are usually eaten for lunch or dinner but they make great breakfast dishes as well.

Tokhum Kachaloo (Eggs with Potatoes)

2 eggs
1-2 tablespoons oil
1 Bell Pepper (Chopped)
1 Onion
1 Potato
1 Tomato
Salt
Pepper
Red crushed pepper

1. Slice onion and sauté in a skillet with oil until transparent on medium low heat.
2. Wash potato, peel and cut in small chunks.
3. Add potatoes to onions, mix with onion and cover the skillet with a lid. Allow to cook on medium low heat until potatoes become tender.
4. In a bowl mix the egg with salt, pepper, and red crushed pepper and add to potatoes.
5. Stir in the egg and mix with onion and potatoes.
6. Chop tomato and bell pepper and add to eggs. Stir and mix with eggs.
7. Cook until eggs are cooked.
8. Serve with bread and green chutney.

Tokhum Gundana (Eggs with leeks)

1 bunch of (Gundana/leeks)
4 eggs
4 tablespoons of oil
salt
pepper

1. Wash gundana thoroughly and cut in small pieces.
2. In a frying pan, add oil and gundana and stir with oil for 5 minutes.
3. In a separate bowl, mix the eggs and add to gundana, along with salt and pepper.
4. Cook until eggs are ready. Serve with bread.

Tokhum Khageena (Egg omelet)

4 eggs
1 onions
1 jalapeno pepper
½ cup of cilantro
¼ of cup of oil
½ cup all purpose flour
salt
pepper

1. Dice onions, jalapeno pepper, and cilantro.
2. In a separate bowl beat eggs until it suds.
3. Add flour, onions, jalapeno peppers, salt, pepper and cilantro to eggs and mix.
4. In a frying pan, heat oil and add the egg mixture.
5. Brown one side and flip to brown other side.
6. Serve with bread.

Tokhum banjan rumi (tomato omelet)

6 eggs
4 Tomatoes
¼ cup of oil
1 medium onion
1 jalapeno pepper
Cilantro (optional garnish)

1. In a frying pan, heat oil.
2. Dice onions and Tomatoes.
3. Add onions to the oil until soft and add tomatoes and cook for 5 minutes on low or until water evaporates.
4. In a separate bowl mix the eggs and add to tomatoes.
5. Dice jalapeno peppers and add to eggs.
6. Add salt and pepper and cook until eggs are ready.
7. Serve with bread.

- Optional: Potatoes and mushrooms can be added to the eggs

Bread and Deserts

Goush-e-feel (Elephant ears)

2 eggs
2 teaspoons sugar
¼ teaspoon salt
½ cup milk
4 teaspoon oil
2 ½ cup plain flour plus ¼ cup for kneading
½ teaspoon ground cardamom
Oil for deep frying

Topping
1 cup confectioner's sugar
½ teaspoon ground cardamom (optional)
½ cup finely chopped pistachio nuts or walnuts.

1. Beat eggs until frothy, beat in sugar and salt. Stir in milk and oil. Sift flour, add half to egg mixture and blend in with wooden spoon. Gradually stir in remainder of flour, holding back about ½ cup.
2. Take mixture out and place on a floured board. Knead for 10 minutes until smooth and glossy, using more flour as needed. Dough will be slightly sticky. Cover with a clean cloth or plastic wrap and allow to sit for about 2 hours.
3. Take a piece of dough about the size of a walnut and roll out on floured board to a circle about 3-4 inches in diameter. Gather up dough on one side and pinch, forming a shape resembling an elephant ear. Place on a cloth and cover. Repeat with remaining dough.
4. Deep fry one at a time in heated oil, turning to cook evenly. Fry until golden brown, but do not over brown. The pastry tends to contract with handling, so just pull out lightly prior to placing in oil.
5. Drain pastries on paper towels.

6. Sift icing sugar with cardamom if used and dust pastries with mixture. Sprinkle with nuts and serve warm or cold

Jillabee

This recipe was kindly given to me by my aunt "Maggie" (Khala Magul). She's the expert Jillabee maker in the family. Jillabee's are delicious deserts that are very sweet and best with tea. The first time I made this, I messed up the syrup and it became too hard and the jillabee stuck together and became hard like rock candy. If you boil the syrup for about 8 minutes and then allow to cool, you can tell the consistency more accurately and adjust it as needed.

1 cup all purpose flour
1 leveled teaspoon dry yeast
8-10 drops of yellow food coloring
1 cup of water
Oil for frying

1. In a bowl, mix flour, yeast, food coloring and water. Use a whisk to mix together for about 1-2 minutes.
2. Cover the bowl and allow to sit for about 15-30 minutes. After 15 minutes, the mixture should be bubbling.
3. Add the mixture in an empty ketchup bottle (refillable condiment bottles) or similar pastry squeeze bag and set aside.

Sugar Base
½ lemon juice
2 ½ cups of sugar
2 cups of water
8-10 drops of yellow food coloring

1. In a saucepan, add sugar and water and allow to boil for about 8-10 minutes.
2. Add ½ lemon juice and mix. Allow to boil for an additional 1-2 minutes.
3. Add 1-2 drops of yellow food coloring and mix.
4. Allow Syrup to cool. (At this point syrup should not be too runny and not too thick. If it is too runny, add ½ cup additional sugar and bring to a boil again and if too thick, add ½ cup of water and boil for 2-3 minutes.) Set syrup aside to cool.

Making the Jillabee
1. In a deep-set frying pan, add 4-5 cups of oil and heat on high. Once oil is heated, lower the heat to medium high.
2. Take the flour mixture and squeeze circular shapes (similar to making a pretzel) in the oil and allow to fry for 1-2 minutes. Dip with a fork to ensure both sides are fried.
3. Remove from oil and dip into sugar mixture for about 1 minute. Use a separate fork for sugar and oil. If the sugar fork touches the oil, it will darken the oil and ruin the jillabee.
4. Remove the jillabee from the sugar mixture and set on a platter. Follow the same procedure for the additional mixture, until mixture is finished.
5. Place the jillabee separately on a platter. Do not set them on top of each other.
6. Serve with tea.

Jillabee

Khajour

This is also a specialty of my aunt Aquila and my aunt Zareen. It is a very delicious desert that is great with tea.

6 eggs
1 ½-2 cups of sugar
5 cups of all-purpose flour
½ cup of milk
¾ cup of oil
1 tablespoon of cardamom
1 teaspoon dry yeast
1 tablespoon baking powder

Oil for frying

1. Mix the sugar, eggs, milk, oil, and cardamom in a bowl.
2. Add flour, yeast, and baking powder to the bowl and mix well. Knead the dough really well, until it becomes elastic. Allow to sit covered for 30-45 minutes (it can sit for up to 10 hours if needed). If dough is thin, you can slowly add about 1 more cup of flour (enough to thicken the dough mixture).
3. Take a piece of the mixture (about the size smaller than a walnut) and roll in your hands and then shape into small rolls.
4. Using the back of a metal colander, press the roll against the back and take your thumb and press in the center to create an indent and thin out the center. Do the same for the rest of mixture.
5. In a skillet, heat 3-4 cups of oil and deep fry the Khajour on medium low heat until browned.
6. Place on a cake rack to drain oil or use a paper towel to absorb the oil on a platter.
7. Serve with tea.

Mehwa-e-Tarkada (Dried Fruit drink)

This is a drink made especially for the Afghan New Year's. Since New Year's Day is the 1ˢᵗ day of Spring, this drink represents Spring, by bringing dried fruit to life by soaking it. It is very delicious and nutritious.

1 lb. of Almonds
1 lb. of Walnuts
1/2 lb. Pistachios (optional)
1/2 lb. of black raisins
1/2 lb. of green raisins
1/2 lb. of dried apricots
3-4 quarts of water

1. In a bowl, add the almonds and the walnuts (and pistachios if desired). Pour hot boiling water over the nuts and allow to soak for 2 days on the countertop.
2. In a separate bowl, add the two different types of raisins and the apricots. Add 3-4 quarts of water over the dried fruit and allow to soak for 2 days in the refrigerator.
3. After a few days, peel the almonds and the walnuts by removing the skin. This can be a very tedious task but it tastes much better without the skin than with it. (If you don't want to peel the nuts, you can soak all the fruit and nuts together for a few days.)
4. After peeling the nuts, mix with the dried fruit and allow to soak for 1-2 days in the refrigerator. The mix should be soupy by this time and juice very sweet.
5. Take fruit mix out of the refrigerator and serve in small bowls or cups.

Halwa-e-Aurd

1 cup vegetable oil
½ cup wheat flour
1 cup all purpose flour
2 ½ -3 cups of sugar
1 ½ cup hot water
1 teaspoon cardamom
1 teaspoon rosewater

1. In a 4 quart pot, add 1 cup oil to ½ cup wheat flour and stir to brown on medium heat.
2. Add ½ cup of all-purpose flour and stir until well mixed. Add additional ½ cup and stir.
3. Add sugar slowly (adjust amount as needed) and stir constantly for 10-15 minutes on medium low heat until flour becomes golden brown.
4. Add hot water and stir for 1 minute.

5. Add cardamom and rose water and stir. Mix well and then wrap lid in a clean cloth, and place on pot. Cook on low for ½ hour.
6. Remove from heat and serve with pita or afghan bread.

Sheer Birinj

1 cup long grain rice (Birinj-e-luk)
3-4 quarts of water
2-2 ½ cups of milk
2 cups of sugar
½ teaspoon of cardamom
1 tablespoon of Rosewater

1. Thoroughly wash rice and soak for about an hour.
2. In a deep pot add water, and drained rice and cook on medium heat for about 40-50 minutes or until the rice kernels are really soft.
3. Lower heat to low setting and add milk and stir constantly.
4. Add rosewater and cardamom and boil for another 1-2 minutes. Stir constantly to make sure the bottom of the pot doesn't stick. The consistency should not be too runny or too thick.
5. When ready, take sheer birinj and put on a deep dish platter. Serve with tea.

- Alternate variation: Substitute water with ¾ milk and ¼ half and half mixture (About a quart of milk to 1 pint of half-and-half ratio). Add rosewater and cardamom and mix well. Place pot in the oven and cook slowly in a 350 degree oven for about an hour. Or you can cook on medium heat on the stove top for about an hour. This is a much richer variation.

Firnee

4 cups of milk
1 cup granulated sugar
½ cup cornstarch
½ cup slivered almonds (optional)
¼ to ½ teaspoon ground cardamom
¼ teaspoon saffron threads (optional)
¼ cup finely chopped pistachio nuts (optional)
2 teaspoons of rosewater

1. Put all but ½ cup of milk into a medium size sauce pan.
2. Take ½ cup of milk and mix with ½ cup of cornstarch.
3. Add milk and cornstarch mix into the pan with the rest of the milk.
4. Over medium heat, stir the mixture constantly until mixture begins to thicken (about 10-15 minutes).
5. (Optional) Add almonds and keep stirring until mixture thickens and bubbles. Use a whisk if mixture becomes lumpy.
6. Add cardamom and rosewater and stir. Cook on low heat for 10 minutes, letting pudding simmer very gently. Stir occasionally.
7. Pour into platter, spreading evenly. Sprinkle pistachio nuts and cardamom around the edge of dish.

Firnee

Rhote

4 cups of white flour
¾ cups of oil
1 egg
1 cup regular milk
2 cups of sugar
1 teaspoon ground cardamom
1 teaspoon baking powder
4-5 tablespoons of dry yeast
Rose water optional

1. Mix flour, oil, eggs, sugar, cardamom, baking powder, and yeast.
2. Heat milk (5-10 seconds in microwave) and add to the mix.
3. Mix all the ingredients and allow to sit in a warm place for 1 hour.
4. Spread on a cookie sheet.
5. Brush 1 teaspoon of oil and ½ teaspoon of milk over the mix.

6. Sprinkle sia dana (nigella) and sesame seeds on top. Cook until brown in a 350 degree oven.

Rhote

Kulcha Khatayee (Almond Cookies)

These cookies are very dry and crumble easily but are very delicious. I first had these cookies at my cousin Harrier's house and absolutely loved them. I craved them for 3 years before I got my hands on the recipe. This is the specialty of my aunt Faiza and uncle Hafiz. I'm grateful that they shared their recipe with me.

5 cups all purpose flour
2 ½ cups sugar
2 ¼ cups oil
1 cup dry milk
½ teaspoon baking soda
1 teaspoon cardamom
1 cup whole almonds
3-4 tablespoons of water

1. Put flour, sugar, oil, milk, baking soda, and cardamom in a bowl and mix really well.
2. Knead dough together until all the ingredients are soft and well mixed. Add water and mix well.
3. Cover bowl and allow to sit for 10-15 minutes.
4. Preheat oven to 350 degrees.
5. Take out a small piece of dough and make walnut size balls. Do this until all the dough is used.
6. Press your thumb in the center of the ball while holding the ball in your hand, supporting the side of the ball.
7. Press 1 almond in the center of the ball and place ball in a flat cookie sheet. Continue with remainder of balls.
8. Place cookie sheet in the oven for 8-10 minutes. Do not leave for longer because they will become too hard.
9. After 10 minutes, take out of oven and allow to cool for 15-20 minutes prior to serving.
10. Serve with tea.

Baklava with Nuts

Syrup:
1 ¾ cups of sugar
1 ½ cups of water
1 teaspoon lemon juice

2-3 tablespoons rose water or orange flower water (optional)

Make the syrup by mixing the water with the 1 ½ cups sugar and bringing it to a boil; simmer 5 minutes. (The amount of sugar can be adjusted according to taste). Add the lemon juice and simmer 5 minutes or more. Cool and add the rose water or orange flower if desired.

1 lb. Blanched almonds, walnuts, pistachios
3 tablespoons sugar
1 cup (2 sticks) sweet, unsalted butter
1 lb. thin phyllo pastry

1. Preheat the oven to 350°. Brush a baking pan (9x13 in.) with butter.
2. Grind the nuts in a blender in parts, by pressing the "chop" button repeatedly about 10-15 times. Then run the blender for a few seconds so that the nuts will be ground but not pulverized. Place the nuts in a mixing bowl; toss with the 3 tablespoons of sugar until well blended. Melt the butter.
3. Unfold the phyllo pastry. Take only one sheet at a time and keep the remaining sheets well covered at all times in order to prevent them from drying out. Place half of one sheet on the bottom of the baking pan and leave the other half draped over the side of the pan. Using a pastry brush, brush the half of the sheet on the pan with butter. Fold the other half of the pastry sheet over the first half; brush it with butter. Repeat this process of layering and buttering the pastry sheets until 7 pastry sheets have been used. Now spread 1/3 of the nut mixture evenly over the sheets in the pan. Add another half sheet of phyllo, brush with butter, and spread another 1/3 of the nut mixture on top. Fold the other half of the sheet, brush it with butter, and spread the remaining nuts over it. Continue layering and buttering the sheets until all the phyllo has been used up. Pour the remaining butter over the top. Press the sheets down gently with your hands or a flat surface. Using a very sharp knife cut the Baklava into diagonal strips 2

inches wide across the pan and cut intersecting diagonal lines to form diamond shapes.

4. Bake 30 minutes at 350°. Reduce the temperature to 300°, place a piece of aluminum foil loosely over the Baklava, and bake 25 minutes longer. Remove from the oven. Tilt the pan and drain off the excess butter if there is any. Pour the cold syrup over the hot Baklava. Let stand several hours. Re-cut the pieces before serving.

Afghan Bread

10 cups of warm water
5 lbs. unbleached white flour
4 cups of whole Wheat flour
3 tablespoons of salt
4 packets of dry yeast
2 tablespoon of sugar
½ cup of vegetable oil
1-2 tablespoons of sesame seeds (optional) or
1-2 tablespoons of sia dana (optional)

1. In a large bowl, mix the white flour, wheat flour, salt, dry yeast, sugar, and oil and add water gradually while kneading the dough until dough is soft yet firm in consistency.
2. Knead dough for 15 minutes consistently. Leave kneaded dough covered for 4-5 hours, or until dough has risen.
3. Then take dough and make balls the size of a saucer plate. Leave covered for 10-15 minutes.
4. Preheat oven to 500 degrees.
5. Take cookie sheets and brush some oil all over the pans.
6. Take dough balls and stretch dough across cookie sheet and poke dough with a butter knife 4-5 times to release trapped air when dough is baking.

7. Sprinkle sesame seeds or sia dana (nigella) if desired and put in oven to bake until brown. Use broil mode in oven to brown the top if desired.
8. Take bread out and brush a little bit of oil on top of bread and take out of pan and put it on the oven rack to cool. Bread is ready to eat.

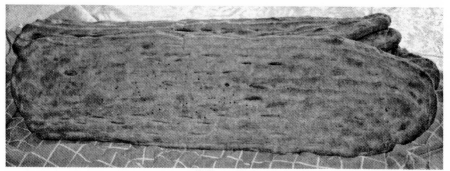

Afghan Bread

Other favorite Deserts (non-Afghan)

Black and White Cheesecake

This is my sister Nahid's specialty. I'm not a fan of cheesecake but I could eat this all day. This cake is a major hit at every gathering she brings it to.

Chocolate Graham Cracker Crust:
1 ½ cups graham cracker crumbs
¼ cup sugar
3 tablespoons cocoa powder
½ cup butter, melted

Filling:
1 ½ pounds cream cheese
1 cup plus 2 tablespoons sugar
2 tablespoons flour
1 teaspoon grated lemon zest
1 teaspoon grated orange zest
3 whole eggs (plus 2 yolks: optional)
½ teaspoon vanilla extract
6 ounces semisweet chocolate, melted
3 tablespoons heavy cream (optional)
½ cup fresh raspberries (optional)

1. Preheat oven to 325 degrees.
2. Toss the crust ingredients together in a bowl. Press firmly into a 10-inch spring form pan, and set aside.
3. Beat the cream cheese and sugar together until light and fluffy.
4. Beat in the flour and zests then slowly beat in the eggs, extra yolks (optional), and vanilla.
5. In a separate bowl, combine the melted chocolate and cream (optional).
6. Pour 2/3 of the cheesecake filling over the crust.
7. Fold the chocolate mixture into the remaining filling until thoroughly combined.

8. Using a knife, swirl the chocolate filling into the plain filling to get a marbled effect.
9. Bake for 40 minutes.
10. Turn off the oven, open the door, and let cake sit for 20 more minutes inside the oven.
11. Cool on a rack.
12. Refrigerate overnight.
13. To make neat slices, cut the cheesecake with a hot knife, rinsing off between each cut.
14. Sprinkle fresh raspberries over the cake and serve

Chocolate Chunk Coffee Cake

This is also my sister Nahid's specialty. This used to be and probably still is my favorite cake. It's absolutely delicious and goes great with tea.

Nut Layer:
1 (4 oz) package Sweet Chocolate, chopped
½ cup chopped nuts
¼ cup sugar
1 teaspoon cinnamon

Cake:
1 ¾ cups all purpose flour
½ teaspoon baking powder
¼ teaspoon salt
1 cup sour cream or plain yogurt
1 teaspoon baking soda
½ cup (1 stick) butter, softened
1 cup sugar
2 eggs
½ teaspoon vanilla
1. Heat oven to 350 degrees F.

2. Mix chocolate, nuts, ¼ cup sugar and cinnamon; set aside.
3. Mix flour, baking powder and salt; set aside.
4. Combine sour cream (or yogurt) and baking soda; set aside.
5. Beat butter and 1 cup sugar in a large bowl until light and fluffy.
6. Add eggs, one at a time, beating well after each addition.
7. Add vanilla.
8. Add flour mixture alternately with sour cream mixture, beginning and ending with flour mixture.
9. Spoon ½ the batter into greased 9-inch square pan.
10. Top with ½ the chocolate-nut mixture, spreading carefully with a spatula. Repeat layers.
11. Bake for 30-35 minutes or until cake begins to pull away from sides of pan. Cool in pan. Cut into squares.

Chocolate Baklava

2 cups slivered almonds, toasted and coarsely chopped
2 cups walnuts, toasted and coarsely chopped
1 ½ cups miniature chocolate chips
1 ½ tablespoons ground cinnamon
½ teaspoon ground cloves
2 ½ tablespoons unsweetened cocoa powder
3 tablespoons butter, melted
Pinch of salt
2 cups of water
2 cups of sugar
3 strips of lemon zest
One 4-inch cinnamon stick
½ teaspoon lemon juice, or to taste
¾ cup honey
1 cup butter, melted
One 1 lb. package phyllo pastry
¼ cup whole cloves
1/3 cup water

1. The Filling: In a food processor coarsely chop the walnuts and almonds.   In a separate bowl or in the food processor, mix together the almonds, walnuts, chocolate chips, cinnamon, cloves, cocoa powder, 3 tablespoons melted butter, and the salt. Set aside at room temperature.

2. The syrup: In a 2 quart saucepan, mix the water, sugar, lemon zest, and cinnamon stick and bring to a boil over high heat. Boil for about 8 minutes or until the mixture thickens to a syrup consistency. Remove the zest and the cinnamon from the syrup and stir in the lemon juice and honey; set syrup aside at room temperature.

3. Preheat the oven to 350 degrees F. Brush a 9x13 inch baking pan with melted butter and lay one sheet of phyllo pastry into the bottom and up the sides of the pan. Brush the phyllo with melted butter and lay a second sheet of phyllo on top. Continue the brushing and layering process until there are 12 layers of buttered pastry. Spread half of the filling over the pastry layers. Smooth the filling evenly, then press it down firmly. Top the filling with 5 more sheets of pastry, brushing each with butter as it is layered. Spread the remaining half of the filling over the pastry, smooth it evenly, and press it down firmly. Top the filling with 12 more sheets of phyllo, brushing each with butter as it is layered. Cut away any pastry that extends up the sides of the baking pan so that the top of the baklava is flat.

4. Using a knife and a ruler cut the baklava into 8 lengthwise strips, cutting all the way through to the bottom of the pan. In the same manner, make a series of parallel cuts diagonally across the first to create diamond shapes. Place a single clove in the middle of each diamond shape and sprinkle the water over the top.

5. Place the baklava in the oven and bake for about 1 hour, or until the pastry is crisp and a rich golden color. Remove the baklava from the oven and pour the syrup evenly over the entire surface of the baklava. Let it stand for at least 30 minutes before eating. Serve at room temperature.

Chocolate Baklava

Chocolate Walnut Tart

1 refrigerated ready to use pie crust
1 cup semisweet chocolate pieces
1 cup coarsely chopped walnuts
¼ cup (½ stick) salted butter
½ cup packed light brown sugar
¾ cup dark corn syrup
3 eggs
1 teaspoon vanilla
Whipped cream (topping) optional

1. Place over rack in lower 3rd of oven. Heat oven to 350 degrees.
2. Unfold the pie crust, roll up on a rolling pin; unroll into 9 inch tart pan with a removable bottom. Fold overhanging crust into pan and press the crust against side of pan. Sprinkle the chocolate and chopped walnuts evenly over the bottom of the pie crust.

3. Microwave the butter in a 4 cup glass measure, covered at 100% power for 40 seconds. Beat in brown sugar, corn syrup, eggs, and vanilla until smooth. Pour evenly into crust.
4. Bake in the lower 3rd of the 350 degree oven for 45 minutes or until the crust is golden brown. Transfer pan to wire rack. Let cool. Remove side of pan. Serve with whipped cream or ice cream as desired.

Chocolate Macaroon Squares (Makes 2 dozen, 2-inch squares)

My sister Nelofer made this at a party one time and we all loved it and begged for the recipe. I don't know where she copied the recipe from but guessing from the recipe, it appears to have been on the Nestle Toll House bag of chocolate morsels.

Topping:
One 14-ounce can sweetened condensed milk
1 teaspoon vanilla extract
1 egg
One 3 ½ -once can (1 1/3 cups) flaked coconut, divided
1 cup chopped pecans
One 6-ounce package (1 cup) Nestle Toll House semi-sweet chocolate morsels

Base:
One 18 ½ -ounce package chocolate cake mix
1/3 cup butter, softened
1 egg

Toping: In a large bowl, combine sweetened condensed milk, vanilla extract, and egg; beat until well blended. Stir in 1 cup coconut, pecans, and semi-sweet chocolate morsels. Set aside.

Base: Preheat oven to 350 degrees F. In a large bowl, combine cake mix, butter, and egg; mix until crumbly. Press into greased 13x9 inch baking pan.

Spread topping over base. Sprinkle remaining 1/3 cup coconut on top. Bake at 350 degree oven for 30-40 minutes.

Note: Center may appear loose but will set upon cooling. Cool completely on wire rack. Cut into 2-inch squares.

Chocolate Chip Cookies

2 cups butter
2 cups sugar
2 cups brown sugar
4 eggs
2 tsp. Vanilla
4 cups flour
1 tsp. Salt (optional)
2 tsp. Baking powder
5 cups oatmeal (put into blender until it turns into powder)
2 tsp. Baking soda
24 oz. (or more) chocolate chips
1 8 oz. Hershey bar, finely grated (can use food processor)
3 cups of chopped nuts

1. Cream together the butter, sugar, and brown sugar.
2. Add eggs (one at a time) and vanilla.
3. Mix together flour, oatmeal, salt, baking powder, and baking soda.
4. Mix together all ingredients.
5. Then add grated Hershey bar, chocolate chips, and chopped nuts.
6. Bake on ungreased cookie sheet at 375 degree (F) oven for 10-13 minutes.

Almond Cake

A light, spongy almond cake moistened with syrup.

Syrup:
3 cups of sugar
2 ½ cups of water
1 teaspoon lemon juice

Dissolve the 3 cups of sugar in the water and bring to a boil. Simmer 10 minutes. Add the lemon juice and simmer 5 minutes longer. Remove from heat and cool.

Cake:
1 ¼ cups almonds, blanched, and ground
1 cup plus 1 tablespoon all-purpose flour (scoop measuring cup into flour and level off with a knife)
10 eggs, at room temperature
½ cup of sugar

1. Preheat the oven to 375°. Toss the ground almonds and flour together in a bowl.
2. Beat the eggs with ½ cup sugar into a thick mayonnaise-like cream; mix in the vanilla. Fold in the flour and almond mixture.
3. Butter a round cake-pan 10 inches in diameter and sprinkle ¼ cup chopped almonds in the bottom. Pour in the batter; sprinkle the remaining almonds on top. Bake 30-35 minutes. Remove from the oven. Pour the syrup over the hot cake. Let it stand until the syrup is absorbed. Serve plain or with whipped cream.

Jams and Marmalades

Quince Marmalade

3 lbs. Quince
4 ¼ cups of water
6 cups sugar
2 tablespoons lemon juice
¼- ½ teaspoon cardamom
Walnuts

Peel the quinces, remove the cores, and seeds, and chop them. Put the chopped quinces in a bowl, cover them with the water, and let them stand overnight. Strain the liquid but save both the fruit and liquid.
Place the liquid in a pan with the sugar; bring to a boil. Add the lemon juice; simmer 10 minutes. Stir in the chopped quince along with cardamom and simmer over low heat about 1 hour. Put a drop of it on a saucer and cool. Tilt the saucer; if the drop does not flow and appears firm, the marmalade is done. If the drop is not firm, cook a little longer. When it is done, bring it to a boil once again, remove from heat, and pour into hot sterilized jars. Seal when the marmalade is cold.

Apricot Jam

3 lbs. of ripe Apricots
1 ½ to 2 cups of water
1 Lemon
6 cups of sugar

1. Wash the apricots, cut in half and remove seeds.
Put apricots in a pot with 1 ¼ cups of water and juice of 1 lemon and boil.
Reduce heat and allow to simmer until fruit is tender. Add extra water as needed.
Allow the contents of the pot to reduce and thicken.

Add sugar and stir until sugar is dissolved.
Increase heat and boil for 10-15 minutes.
Pour into warmed clean jars and allow to cool. Then seal jars and store in a cool dry place or refrigerate.

Blackberry Jam

I learned this recipe while in Humboldt from one of my friends. Humboldt has a large supply of Blackberry bushes, and during the summer, we'd go out there with our long gloves and pick the sweet, ripe blackberries and make jam. Picking blackberries is one of the hardest tasks because you get cut up by the thorns on the branches. You also get stained by the berries so wear very dark clothing while picking blackberries.

3 lbs. blackberries
¼ cup of water
2 lemons
6 cups sugar

1. Thoroughly clean the blackberries by removing sticks and other debris. Rinse gently and place in a pot with the water and juice of 2 lemons and bring to a boil.
2. Reduce the heat to medium-low and simmer until the berries are cooked and the syrup begins to thicken.
3. Add the sugar and stir until dissolved.
4. Increase heat to high and allow to boil for 10-15 minutes.
5. Remove any crust or foam from top and pour into warmed glass jars.
6. Cover and allow to cool.
7. Place in a cool dry place or refrigerate.
8. Best used on cream cheese.

Cherry Jam

5 lbs. Cherries
3 lemons
7 cups of sugar
¼ cup of water

1. Wash cherries and remove pits.
2. Place cherries in a pot with juice of 3 lemons and water.
3. Turn heat on medium high and slowly bring to a simmer as you stir the cherries occasionally. Simmer until cherries are tender.
4. Add sugar and stir until dissolved.
5. Increase heat to high and bring to a boil. Boil for 10-15 minutes.
6. Remove the scum from top and pour Jam into warmed glass jars.
7. Cover and allow to cool.
8. Store in a cool dry place or refrigerate.

Dried Fig Jam

I learned this recipe from the Preserves and Pickles book (see Appendix) many years ago.

2 lbs. dried figs
3 ¾ cups of water
6 tablespoons lemon juice
6 cups white sugar

1. Place the figs in a bowl with water to cover; soak for at least 12 hours.
2. Drain the figs and rinse them in fresh water.
3. Cut out the stem and chop roughly.
4. Place in a cooking pot with the water and lemon juice.
5. Bring to a boil and simmer gently until the figs are tender.
6. Add sugar and stir until dissolved.

7. Boil rapidly until the contents of the pot have thickened.
8. Pour the hot jam into hot clean jars. Cover.

Raspberry Jam

This recipe is also from the Preserves and Pickles book (see Appendix).

3 lbs. raspberries
6 cups of sugar

1. Clean berries carefully and place in a pot.
2. Heat gently on medium until some of the juice has come out.
3. Simmer until the raspberries are softened and tender.
4. Add sugar and stir until dissolved.
5. Increase heat to medium high and boil rapidly for 10-15 minutes.
6. Remove the scum on top and pour the hot jam in to the hot clean jars. Cover.

Seedless Raspberry Jam: Follow recipe above to step 3 and then press the cooked raspberries through a sieve and discard the seeds. Make sure that all the pulp and juice is returned to the rinsed cooking pan before adding sugar.

Strawberry Jam

This recipe is also from the Preserves and Pickles book (see Appendix). This is a difficult jam to make due to the low pectin level of the strawberries but the lemon juice, pith, and rind add extra pectin to the jam.

3 ½ lb. Strawberries
2 lemons (juice, pith, and rind)
6 cups of white sugar

1. Hull the strawberries and place them in the cooking pan with the lemon juice, the lemon rind, and pith tied in a muslin bag.
2. Heat gently, stirring until the juice begins to run.
3. Simmer until the fruit is tender and the contents of the pan are reduced.
4. Add the sugar and stir until dissolved.
5. Increase heat and boil rapidly for 10-15 minutes.
6. Remove the scum from the jam immediately and then allow it to cool slightly before pouring into hot jars.
7. Cover when cold.

• Whole Fruit Strawberry Jam: Take 3 ½ lb. Strawberries and place them (hulled) in a pot with 6 cups of sugar. Heat gently, stirring constantly, until the sugar is dissolved. Add 1 ¼ cup of red currant juice and boil rapidly for 10-15 minutes. Follow steps 6-7 above.

Appendix

Saberi, H., *Afghan Food and Cookery.* New York: Hippocrene Books, Inc., 2000.

Burt, A., *Preserves and Pickles.* London: Octupus Books Limited, 1973.

Algar, A.E., *The Complete Book of Turkish Cooking.* New York: Kegan Paul International, 1985.

Freke, E., *The Complete Book of Spices.* London: New Burlington Books, 1997.

Keville, K., *Herbs for Health and Healing.* Pennsylvania: Rodale Press, Inc., 1996.

Brody's, J., *Good Seafood Book.* New York: W.W. Norton & Company, 1994.

About the Author

Nafisa Sekandari was born and raised in Afghanistan until the age of nine, at which point her family was forced to escape Afghanistan after the Soviet Invasion. In December of 1979, Nafisa and her family moved to the United States and lived in Virginia until 1984, at which point, they moved to California. This book is the result of many years of collecting, research, observation, and practice in regards to cooking Afghan cuisine. Nafisa is currently a practicing School Psychologist and a Licensed Educational Psychologist in the Northern California San Francisco Bay Area. It is the intention of this author to send a portion of the proceeds of this cookbook to help the women and children in Afghanistan with needs such as education, healthcare, and nutrition. For feedback regarding the book, please contact the author at nafisasekandari2002@yahoo.com.

Printed in the United States
39894LVS00006B/127-132

9 781403 385901